P9-CDK-659

Bobby
Wonderful

Also by Bob Morris

Assisted Loving: True Tales of Double Dating with My Dad
Crispin the Terrible

Bobby Wonderful

An Imperfect Son Buries His Parents

BOB MORRIS

TWELVE

New York   Boston

Twelve

Hachette Book Group

1290 Avenue of the Americas

New York, NY 10104

www.HachetteBookGroup.com

Printed in the United States of America

RRD-C

First Edition: June 2015

10 9 8 7 6 5 4 3 2 1

Twelve is an imprint of Grand Central Publishing. The Twelve name and logo are trademarks of Hachette Book Group, Inc.

The Hachette Speakers Bureau provides a wide range of authors for speaking events. To find out more, go to www.hachettespeakersbureau.com or call (866) 376-6591.

The publisher is not responsible for websites (or their content) that are not owned by the publisher.

Library of Congress data has been applied for.

ISBN 978-1-4555-5650-2 (Hardcover ed.);
ISBN 978-1-4789-0391-8 (Audiobook downloadable ed.);
ISBN 978-1-4555-3014-4 (Ebook ed.)

To Jeff, my loving and protective big brother,
whose devotion to family is a daily blessing,
challenge, and inspiration.

Bobby Wonderful

Ashes: A Prelude

Just before Christmas a few years ago, I met a man at a holiday party who was ecstatic after seeing a major ballet company's performance of *The Nutcracker*. His mother's ashes, he told me and a few others gathered around him, had been used as the snow on the set—sprinkled in with the usual fake stuff covering the floor—and the remainder had been dumped into a box with the rosin that dancers use on their toe shoes. None of them, of course, knew about it.

"She loved ballet so much," he said. "It was the perfect ending."

One man's perfect ending is another's gruesome one, I guess. My family has never been the cremating kind. But as the exuberant man went on to explain how the strange occurrence had come to be—the artistic director of the ballet company had known his eccentric mother, who was a fan—and how happy he was that he had been able to show her out with such panache, I started thinking about the conventional burials of both my relatively conventional parents.

Then I thought about my own engagement with them in the last years before they died.

When this man's mother became infirm, he told me, he moved her into his small house in a tiny Virginia town without a second thought. He rallied the entire block not just to befriend her but to show up to amuse her and help him help her as she languished. This busy man, a media specialist with a passion for the advocacy work that sends him around the world, didn't think twice when the time came to take his mother in and make her a major part of his hectic life.

"I loved her and I wanted to do the best I could for her, that's all," he said.

His cheeks were red from the beer he was drinking and the warmth of the party. He wasn't mourning at all, it seemed. Rather, he was joyful and triumphant, and also, of course, relieved to be done with the wrenching and prolonged process of helping a loved one die.

"It was hard, but I learned so much from doing it," he said.

He even made a reluctant adolescent niece go in and look at his mother in her last days.

"I told her getting old isn't pretty but it's important to see," he said.

He talked and talked, and I listened without saying a word. With my own parents and their last years, there were so many moments of aggravation, anxiety, and despair, but rarely the triumphs that this lively man was able to find with his mother at the end of her life. When people speak about a "good death," it can mean many things. It seemed he had provided her with an excellent one, right down to what could only be described as a showstopping finale.

And what had I done for my mother? I wasn't helpful as an advocate with her doctors—I left that to my assertive older brother. And I wasn't all that present (at least in my mind) at the end of her life, or at the end of my father's life either, even though they were nearby. My father even had to shame me into visiting him more often and for longer amounts of time, which I found both infuriating and mortifying. Much as I loved him, the old man could get to me right to the end. He could not bear any criticism, but he was full of advice, regardless of his lack of expertise in any given area. If I had moved in with him as he'd once suggested, we would have both ended up dead. He was, after all, a mess-making and willful character who didn't follow the simplest instructions and would talk the ear off anyone inclined to listen. My mother was easier and more contained, but she had her issues too, including such a fear of any kind of risk taking that she would cancel plans at the slightest chance of inclement weather. She was doting, but not at all amusing like the exuberant mother who ended up in *The Nutcracker*. Shameful as it is to admit, neither of my parents was what I'd have ordered from a parent catalogue. And yet they were so good to me; they loved me so much, even more than each other.

They deserved so much more than what I gave them in their last years.

Why does it bug me so much that I didn't do enough for them? Is that something most sons and daughters tend to feel around parents? I still feel it today, with mine both long gone.

Saying good-bye to the parents. Facing their last years, if not with valor, then at least with humor and equanimity. It's a topic that seems to come up all the time now, as much a matter of demographics as a strange new urgency of the boomer generation to process everything in public. Our parents are living longer due to advances in gerontology, and it throws us up against questions about how to help them out without totally sacrificing the quality of our own lives.

When we take away their car keys, does it mean we have to be their drivers? If we think their cognitive abilities are failing, do we have to take them for tests that might make life more difficult for everyone? One elderly mother I know is able-bodied and on the ball. Always well put together, she loves company and opines on politics with the energy of a college-age liberal. I think she's remarkable. Her loving, middle-aged children are often too worried about her health to see how well she's actually doing. They debate with her and each other about what's best, and don't always agree.

Not long ago a friend was telling me about his father's dementia. Still in his seventies, the father had to live in a nursing home, expensive but necessary. My friend's carefully composed mother could barely deal with her husband and his chaotic mind. It was the same with my friend's younger sister, who claimed too much on her plate with her job and a young child.

"It's a total disaster, and none of us know what to do," my friend told me.

Money was one of the most serious concerns. They were a family without much of a financial cushion, and they were watching what little they had vanish to service a dying man who didn't even seem to know where he was, let alone care.

I found myself asking lots of questions. I wanted to know if the demented father was physically strong. I wanted to know if "comfort care," code for using enough morphine to gently extinguish all suffering and eventually the heart-beat itself, had been discussed. There were no easy answers, and my friend and his family felt lost in a situation they could barely navigate.

"What if he goes on like this for years?" my friend asked. "Is it horrible for me to actually think we'd all be better off if he died right away instead?"

I knew what he was feeling because I had the same thoughts during my mother's devastating last years. She was just so sick, what was the point of going on?

"I don't think it's horrible to think anything, just honest," I finally said.

Another friend, who watched his dynamo grandmother

languish in a nursing home for her last five years, and was appalled to see her go that way, put it like this when talking about his idea of an ideal ending for his still-healthy parents: "In ten years, they'll be coming home from one of their fabulous Paris trips, and their Air France flight will go down over the Atlantic. That will save us all from the kind of humiliation and suffering my grandmother had to endure."

Brutal? Yes. Understandable? Yes, that too.

Caring for parents has become the new normal for boomers. It is estimated that 65 million people in this country are caregivers, with seven out of ten of them looking after someone over the age of fifty. Many of these caregivers report depression and some a decline in health. Most aren't the perfect and selfless children who want to move their parents in with them and have their ashes scattered at a ballet. And they don't have the vision to see what only the selfless and enlightened can know when in the middle of it, and what I only know now that the experience is behind me, making it easy to say: Caring for your parents is an opportunity.

Last fall, in the course of not much more than a month, five of my friends posted on Facebook about the deaths of their fathers. (Ten years ago, that would not have been possible, and neither would the opportunity to comment on or "like" the news.) I'd met many of these deceased fathers in passing while in college. How strange and yet completely in the order of things that these powerful and successful men had weakened and then reached their ends.

At a recent memorial service I attended for the dapper stepfather of one friend, it was disconcerting to see my peers looking so middle-aged. But that wasn't half as disturbing as seeing all the friends and colleagues of the deceased—my parents' generation. Healthy people who had always lived at the top of their games were teetering from the chapel to the reception—women unsteady on low heels, men walking with crooked backs. A population in decline.

"It must be so strange for them to go to so many friends' funerals," an acquaintance observed. "I bet they're thinking about what their own will be like in the months ahead."

And I have to admit, I was thinking along the same lines. Will I have any friends around to attend a service for me? What would they say if they were to speak? Would my Manhattan friends—those who would still be alive—show up at the family cemetery on Long Island? Would I even want them to bother figuring out how to get there, since many of them don't drive? At least I don't have to worry anyone about my outfit, since Jews don't do open caskets. But one man I know, an Episcopalian, was packing up the house of his mother in the days after her death when the undertaker called to ask what she wanted to be wearing for her funeral. The son had no idea and panicked as he went through the dresses in her closet and tried to choose one. In the morning, the doorbell rang—it was a delivery from a high-end mail-order catalogue. Inside was a cheerful summer dress that his mother had chosen weeks earlier for the occasion. "I had to laugh," he said. "My mother was always the type to think of everything."

How did any of us become old enough to see things like this? It's hard to imagine because we're a generation so adamant about maintaining our youth. And like us, our parents are pushing the boundaries too. They are fit and vital and not about to let anyone shove them aside. I mean, when he was eighty and my mother had not even been gone for half a year, my father asked me for dating advice. He even asked me to escort him on some of his dates. His year of active romancing, with me along for the ride acting as something between his wingman and his pimp, turned out to be the best year of our lives together. When I sold his sedan after his death at age eighty-three, I found an unused condom in his glove compartment. I like to tell people that he was always a very hopeful man.

Many people have stories of escapades with senior parents. This, in part, is why it shocks us when they're really at the end. And it's why I put together this personal chronicle of ending. Much as we want to suppress our less-than-honorable thoughts in the presence of ailing parents, those thoughts are there. Mine still haunt me years later. But then, the death of a parent is a life-changing situation, dramatic as giving birth in some ways. Do we just go through the motions at the very end and then force ourselves to move on too quickly? Or do we take the time, as one friend did, to visit her ailing father as much as she could in his last year? She got him to his beloved golf course in a wheelchair at the end and let him give her a lesson. She played a prelude on the piano for him, a lilting and sweet one by Bach. It made him cry. From his bed he made her lean in close, and he sang a song to her from *Carousel* about a young father's hopes for a daughter. When he died, she didn't rush back from Michigan to New York City. She stayed; she slept in the family house and revisited the places of her childhood. She visited the graves of her parents every day. She took naps by them. She made sure the flowers looked beautiful. She lingered until it was time for her to rejoin the world.

It took a while before my mother and father started showing up in my dreams, but now I see them all the time. I was dreaming of playing tennis and turned to find that my father was my doubles partner, as he was for decades, but as an old man who, as if by magic, could play as well as he did when he was a young tournament champion. He told me, as he always did, to toss the ball higher when I served. Recently I dreamed that my mother, cocooned in a blanket on our old living room couch, stood up to hug me. At first I was chagrined that I had been talking to my father and I hadn't even noticed her there. Then I was overjoyed at her embrace.

She was laughing. She was alive again. "It's all a wonderful game, isn't it," she whispered to me.

It is often said that the death of someone important in your life doesn't necessarily mean the relationship is over, just that it's in a new phase. I still have conversations with both my parents when I visit their graves. I still remember to thank them every time I find myself somewhere beautiful, whether at a concert hall, in a foreign city, or looking out over a breathtaking view from a sailboat or mountaintop. And I still have doubts all the time about how I treated them in their last years.

Death, I often thought as I went through the process of helping my parents depart this world, is as much about the needs of those helping and bearing witness as of those who are dying.

Death, I still often think as I watch my friends help their parents die, is for the living.

Back at the holiday party, the exuberant son was telling more people the story of the extravagant use of his mother's ashes in *The Nutcracker*. Each time he told it, people laughed and shook their heads in amazement. It was an unbeatable send-off, beyond anyone's imagination and the ultimate personalization of death in a society of people obsessed with originality. What a triumph. I listened to him talk about it each time as if I hadn't heard it before. It was so funny, but also so complicated, emotional, and resonant.

"It was better than anything I could have imagined," he said.

The night was clear when I left the party.

But in my head a pale flurry of ashes and memories was falling from the sky, delicate, silent, and blanketing the December night.

Mom

The Wicked Son

A warm late-summer wind blows through the golden barley fields on the hillsides. They seem to shimmer in the sun as I step into a phone booth outside a medieval village in the Highlands of Scotland. It's August 2002 and I don't have a global cell phone, but I want to talk to my mother, who's in the hospital in New York. I've been meaning to call for several days now. It isn't easy, but I charge the call to a credit card and a stranger's voice answers.

"Mom?"

"Who is this?"

"Who is *this*?" I shoot back.

"Her nurse's aide."

"This is Bob, her son, can you put her on?"

I wait a moment, unable to appreciate the rolling landscape all around me because I feel so anxious and far from home. My mother, seventy-three and desperately infirm from a blood disease that has been taking her down for years and now seems to be pushing her to her final months, fell from her bed and hit her head on the day I left New York City for a Scotch-tasting tour. I struggled with getting on the plane, but in the end, I couldn't resist, and off I went.

"Mom?"

What I hear doesn't sound like my mother, who was lucid several days ago.

"Ahhh! Aaaah!"

"Mom, how are you?" I ask.

"Aaaah," she bleats again. I can hear the aide telling her it's me, her son Bob. After my mother makes more disconcerting noises, the aide comes back on the line.

"What's happening?" I ask.

"We're not sure," the aide says. "Your father told me he wants you to call him at home."

I'm sweating now, hands damp as I grip the phone and look around. This landscape is kind of like Vermont but with castles. It hasn't impressed me that much, certainly not enough to have brought me all this way when my mother sounds so terrible.

"Is it her brain? What is it?"

"You can ask your father. I have to go."

Then she hangs up. I do too, and put my palm on my damp forehead. I thought before I left that my mother would recuperate from her fall. She was in bad shape, but it didn't seem she would die from it. So when I halfheartedly mentioned canceling this trip, my father and my older and only brother, Jeff, told me to go and enjoy myself. At least that's what I thought I heard.

Well, I've already spent plenty of time with her the whole sad summer. This trip, for which I have my family's moral clearance, is supposed to be a break from the worry around her rapid unraveling. But I feel lost all these miles away. I call my father at home. The line is busy. The sunlight shoots across the hillside into my red phone booth, which is rusted in parts, with a dusting of soil on the metal floor. On one ridge beyond a field, a herd of sheep—sweaters on the hoof—cross into shadows cast by trees. The hills move like wind-tossed seas of golden hops, rye, and barley—Scotch and beer ingredients ready for the reaping. I thought Scotland would be wilder, somehow. But the scene is disappointingly tame.

I call my father again and this time it rings. He picks up. He's always happy when I call.

"Nice to hear from you," he says. He always says that, and he means it.

"Hi, Dad. What's with Mom? She doesn't sound so good."

"She's coming along, but it might take a few more days," he says.

"Why does she sound like that?"

"We're not sure. We're trying to find out."

"Really? It's weird. Don't you think?"

"Listen, don't let it worry you, just enjoy your trip."

Am I talking to the husband of a woman he's been married to for fifty years? Is my father really so sanguine, or is he just trying to tell me what I want to hear while on vacation?

"I'm wondering if I should come back early."

"When is your trip supposed to end?"

"In five days. Is that okay?"

"Well, you don't want to spoil your vacation. How is it over there?"

"It's fine—we're staying in castles and dressing up for dinners."

"Sounds up your alley. You should stay and enjoy. Anyway, this call is long distance. It must be costing you a fortune. Why don't you check in again in a few days? I'm sure she'll be able to talk to you by then."

"You really think so, Dad?"

"Absolutely."

My father has always been a loopy optimist. Both irresponsible and irrepressible, he can't manage my mother's pill schedule or much of anything else. Yet he has stayed by her side for the past dozen years, watching her get to her current skeletal state, her once-pretty face now a sharp hatchet wedge. And he still sings to her and brings her cheesecake from highway diners and candy from the bridge luncheons he attends while she languishes at home, barely able to turn the pages of the newspaper. Can I blame him for living his life? Maybe, but I empathize too. He wants to have fun. So do I. My brother, a couple of years old than me, with a successful business, a lovely family, and two big homes (one in the city, one in the exurbs), has always been the good son and the family's morality meter. I've always been more the wicked one, the boy we learn about at our Passover Seder each spring—prodigal, cynical, and irresponsible.

But cavalier as I'd like to be, this trip isn't working out. And although it seems absurd to complain about such luxury, the formal meals are becoming overbearing as we shlep all over the country in a jet-lagged state, from one distillery to the next. Worst of all, I get no chance, with the time difference, to call my family. I get back from my Scotch-soaked dinners each night too drunk to figure out the phones, let alone talk. Our inns are old and without easy Internet access.

Yet part of me still believes I deserve to be here after doing service all summer with my mother, spending every Tuesday with her so my father can run around. I've played piano for her, played Scrabble with her, lifted her in and out of bed. But it's possible that no amount of Scotch-drinking—and I've done my share these past few days—can medicate away the harsh and confusing truth our family is facing now. She's a sinking wreck with no firm end in sight.

I leave the phone booth to walk in the late-afternoon sun, crossing over a clear gurgling stream on a bridge of gray stone, and through a quiet village down narrow cobbled streets, and then onward to the castle turned into an inn where I have to dress for another black-tie dinner. The outfit I put on almost feels like it's for mourning. But I know I'm very privileged to be here to partake of such fine things, even if they aren't exactly as I had imagined. I want to enjoy it more. I want the scenery to uplift as the Scotch sedates. I don't want to be critical of everything all the time. I want to be more appreciative of life—the way my parents would want me to be.

On Islay, an island in the south known for its smoky (peaty, in the parlance) single-malt Scotches, I step out of our grand old hotel one night onto a golf course that rolls down to the sea. It is very late, so late that the summer sunset has finally wiped the horizon to a smudged blackboard gray. In the sky to the north I see something I don't understand, a kind of gauzy pulsing. There's no city there or in any direction anywhere near this remote place, and there are no clouds, so it can't be lightning either. Then it hits me that I'm seeing the northern lights, soft as the splotches and streaks you see when you close your eyes. They instantly remind me of a favorite memory, one I return to again and again to hold my mother in my mind during these dark years of illness. We were a young family on Lake Erie near Buffalo one summer at a motel, my brother and me in one bed, my parents in the other. I was nine, intent on making her happy.

I must have seen the glow through the bathroom window, something astonishing to a boy from Long Island, where the only wash of light in the sky is the chemical pink from New York City. Had we heard news of the aurora borealis that week? I can't remember. But I do remember trying to wake everyone to join me outside. My brother and father barely stirred and would not leave their beds. My mother got up right away in her summery nightgown.

We stood outside in front of the motel room, holding hands and looking up beyond the trees at the subtle glow of the light show in the sky. I could feel her wedding and engagement rings, the ones I knew so well from playing old-timey duets with her on the piano. We watched the sky in silence, with the roar of the interstate and the drone of cicadas the only soundtrack.

It was late. I rubbed my eyes, not wanting to go back to bed. We both yawned.

"You always find the most beautiful things to show me," she said.

Well, I tried. In later years I introduced her, the innocent suburban librarian, to foreign films and writers she'd never have known. But then, I was as pretentious a young man as she was unassuming. And as a boy I wanted to play her the sweetest songs and make her the best cards for birthdays and holidays. I wanted to get the highest grades for her too. She delighted in all of it, as I loved her voice, the way she wore her hair and dressed. She was a good mother, maybe even a magnificent one, never self-absorbed like other mothers I'd hear about when I got to college and found myself among far wealthier and more sophisticated sons and daughters.

On sunny Saturdays, when other neighborhood boys were out playing baseball or climbing trees, and my brother and father were off on a tennis court somewhere, she and I would sit in a sunspot in the den, with me half in her lap and half off. I was still young enough for physical affection, but just barely. She'd stroke my hair and hum. I'd nip her arm.

"My little tiger cub," she'd say.

Our breathing felt like it was in unison.

I don't embrace her like that anymore. Perhaps I should, but I don't know how. She is so fragile, so bony and prone to shouting "Ouch!" when touched the wrong way. I've been doing what I can to help her find tiny moments of pleasure. But the walks are too much effort. The music on the car stereo that I think she'll like is too loud. Only when I play the piano (which my brother thoughtfully had moved from our parents' Long Island house to their new assisted living apartment, conveniently located around the corner from his city duplex) can I reach her.

My fingers touch the ivory keys I've known since childhood and that I always play with all the feeling I can find. I have been doing this for decades, even in my thirties when I returned for a time to live at home. I would often play "Look for the Silver Lining." Her voice from her kitchen would carry across the living room, decorated in her symphony of blues—navy, royal, and aquamarine—her favorite colors.

Whenever clouds appear in the blue

I played the same song the night before I left for this trip. She was lying on the bed in the next room. I wondered if it would be my last time playing it for her. Her singing was so soft and raspy. She was working so hard to get the words out—as she had worked so hard for so long to be a good mother and wife, and then later to be of good cheer before the illness made her finally collapse in despair. She kept singing that last night, and I forced myself to keep playing.

I can't stop hearing that song as I stand here now in the northern night of a Scottish summer, too far from home, guilty, angry, and afraid.

Remember somewhere the sun is shining

The lights in the sky pulse almost as if to the rhythm of the song, our song. I take in a long breath and let it out. She would have loved this sky just as she loved every sunset, every full moon, and the first blossoms of April in our suburban town.

"I'm sorry, Mom," I say.

As the tour goes on, each new charming distillery we visit, with the copper stills, oak barrels, test tubes for blending, and family histories of owners told in elegant Scottish accents, annoys more than it impresses. It doesn't help that my fellow travelers are testy too, sick of the smell of fermenting rye and tired of dressing for dinner. One night, I get back to our hotel in Inverness, a pleasant town of green lanes, waterways, and gardens, to find a message at my door.

Your sister-in-law from New York: Please call her as soon as possible.

Uh-oh, I think. *Things have gotten worse back home.*

"Your brother is upset," she tells me the next morning when I reach her. "He doesn't understand why you haven't called him to check on your mother."

"I'm on the road all day. But he could have called me."

"He tried. But really, you should be the one picking up the phone to call."

I feel my defenses shoot up, as they often do around my brother.

"I don't have access to phones every day," I bark. "And I don't have access to e-mail."

"Look, I understand, I really do," says my sister-in-law, who has found herself in the position of the messenger before, and is kind to step in. "But I'm just telling you to talk to him."

I say, "Okay, okay, I got it, thank you," and hang up and let out a long sigh.

"Listen," my brother says when I reach him moments later, "I don't know what you're doing or what you're thinking. I guess you don't want to hear about anything that might ruin your trip, but Mom is in terrible shape and we're with her all day and night at the hospital now."

"I had no idea it's been like that," I say.

"You talked to Dad, and you know what's going on."

"But he told me not to come home."

"That's Dad, he'd never tell you to ruin your fun."

I feel my foot tapping beneath the sleek glass table in my hotel's business center. I feel my palms go sweaty. It's true. My father will rarely let responsibility spoil the fun. My brother is the one whose standards for how we should treat each other are so admirably high that at times he can make me squirm, squawk, and spin out like a rear wheel in the mud.

"So what do you want me to do? Buy a ticket to come home early?"

"If you want to see her alive, you should get on a plane tomorrow."

"Are you mad at me?"

"I just think you should be home."

"I'm sorry," I say. "I wish you had figured out a way to tell me this sooner."

"I left a message."

"I never got it."

"And I really expected you to be in touch."

Here we go again, I'm thinking. I love him so much. But I will always disappoint him. When he graduated from college, I couldn't be bothered to fly home from California to attend the ceremony. When he turned thirty and my parents threw him a big party, it was the same thing. I just can't always be bothered to do right by him, and it creates a turbulent dynamic, a constant tugging and testing. I call him judgmental, although I'm quicker to pass judgment on people than anyone. He suggests that my default mode is irresponsible and selfish. He jokes that I'm a quitter because as a kid I didn't finish playing board games, including, he likes to point out with some irony, The Game of Life. He isn't wrong, but that doesn't mean I want to hear it. And I do tend to abandon card games, Scrabble, and tennis matches the moment I get bored, the same way I do writing projects. Now he is making me defensive and furious about our mother, whom he showers with the kind of extravagant care and concern that I could never give.

"I just want you to know I already said my good-byes when I left for this trip," I tell him with what sounds like the yelp of a trapped animal. "I wasn't sure she'd make it."

"She might not. But I can promise that if you don't get back here soon, you could end up full of regret and talking about it in therapy for the rest of your life."

Then he clicks off and I'm hit by a dial tone.

"Therapy?" I say to myself. "Since when does anyone in our family do therapy?"

And then something else occurs to me: My brother loves my mother more than I do. He would do anything for her— he and his wife have taken her and my father on trips to Europe, hosted them for countless long weekends, lavished her with gifts she would never buy for herself. I love him for it, even if it raises the bar so high that it makes me feel inadequate. Who could ever match his caring? He'll always be the better son. He'll always go beyond the call of duty.

I step into the lobby of the hotel we've moved to in Glasgow, the first modern one we've stayed in all week, with computers and easy phone access. Tourists and businesspeople come and go around me. I am shaking with something between shame and rage as I call my father. I tell him what my brother said and that I won't be shamed by him. But I am very much ashamed.

"Who does he think he is? Why does he have to make me feel so guilty all the time?"

"Jeff has very high standards, we know that," my father says.

"I don't need him deciding for me what I should and shouldn't do."

"Listen, Bobby," he says. "The most important thing right now is that we get along, that we all do what we can to pull together as a family and do what's best for Mom, that's all."

"Yes, you're right," I say.

"Jeff can't say it, but he needs you now," Dad says. "He needs you home. We all do."

It is uncharacteristically wise, eloquent even, and I thank him and tell him he's right and that I'll do what I can. Then I call my airline about a flight home. There are none the next day, but I can get one on Sunday, a day earlier than the rest of the group, for $500—discounted by half for the emergency. It's a lot of money to me. And it takes a while to commit to it over the phone. When I hang up, I find myself thinking I'm glad I have one more day in Scotland.

I have always wanted to see Edinburgh, and the next day I roam from cafés to abbeys and to windswept streets high up over the North Sea. Near Edinburgh Castle I find a chic woolens shop. I want to buy something for my mother, but the hundred dollars for a pure Shetland scarf is too expensive. It isn't just that I'm not good at spending money on gifts, it's this awful question of whether she will be in her right mind to appreciate any kind of gift at all. Or will she even be alive? I find a scarf for half the price. It has stripes of blue, her favorite color.

It's already late afternoon by the time I walk into her uptown hospital, a looming building with an airy atrium for a lobby. I got home the night before but wanted to unpack and settle in before throwing myself into the family crisis. I guess it was negligent. Maybe even egregiously so. I rushed home only to take my time in getting to her.

When I find her room on the tenth floor, instead of the emaciated but completely lucid mother I said good-bye to a week ago, I see a deranged one, a pale mass of agitation, hooked up to tubes and writhing in bed. The sound she makes is a kind of caterwauling, like a fussy infant who can't get comfortable. For some reason a nurse has put lipstick on her, a gash of red on her lips that has smeared onto her teeth. It makes her seem even more alien. Dad and Jeff look up at me and nod. I hold up a hand in greeting.

"Look, Mom, it's Bobby," says Jeff, whose face is tight with worry.

"He's home now, Ethel," adds my father, so rested-looking that it seems unfair.

We don't hug each other in greeting. It seems irrelevant. I just go to her bedside and take her hand. For the briefest of moments, she becomes still and her eyes stop on my face. In them I can still see the woman I once thought was the most beautiful mother in the world.

"Bobby," she says.

At least I think that's what she says. Or maybe it's what I want to believe she is saying. The truth is, it's impossible to understand anything that comes out of her. Something terrible and unknowable has happened since she fell last week and banged her head. The doctors have been saying it's just a hematoma, a bruise. How could that cause someone to become like this?

I present her with my gift, wrapped and in a box from Edinburgh. She can't even take it from me. I leave it on her chest for a moment, then take it back.

"Can I unwrap it for you?" I ask.

I do, and pull out the modest striped blue scarf and hold it up for her to see.

"Look, Mom, it's from Scotland and it's your colors."

My father leans in to look. Maybe he's hoping this gift will rouse her from her state.

"It matches your eyes, Ethel," he says.

I knew it would. I want to wrap her in it, thinking maybe it will make her feel better—it's chilly in the air-conditioned

room—but she's hooked up to too many tubes. So I leave it
by her head next to her pillow. Under her sheets, she keeps
shifting around, her shape changing like sand dunes in a
windstorm. Jeff is quiet. We talked on the phone when I got
back and smoothed things over as much as we could. As the
crisis manager on behalf of our mother, he has more on his
mind than me. He tells me her doctor is due in a little while.
We will find out the result of this test or that one, but even
he knows there's little left to be done. Meanwhile, he asks
about my trip. I don't want to talk about it. I'm ashamed it's
the reason I stayed away. And there's nothing to say except
that all that Scotch and luxury has left a medicinal aftertaste.

My father looks at my brother and then at me.

"Come on. Tell us about your trip. Mom would like to
hear, wouldn't you, honey?"

Of course. Because that's what we have to do, regardless
of whether someone can understand a word of what we're
saying. We talk to them in hospital beds, we tell them things
and hope we can bring them back to us. My job in the family is to lighten and to entertain. It's how I contribute as the
irresponsible son. So I talk about my trip. And as I do, I
remember trips I've told her about when she was such a fierce
listener, always delighted to hear everything.

Papua New Guinea, Guatemala, South Africa, India,
Mexico. Each time, I'd come home from exotic travel magazine assignments and tell her about them, like a child back
from school or camp. My father paid only so much attention

to my tales before a ball game or phone call would distract him. But she was always rapt. "You have such an interesting career," she'd say.

I didn't always think so. I was lonely much of the time, and frustrated that I wasn't getting all the work I wanted. But I loved the look in her eyes when I'd tell her about my trips.

The last time I told her about one was on Mother's Day. I showed up from the city at their house on Long Island to take them out to brunch. My father was in a bad mood. I didn't understand why until I realized he didn't want to leave his baseball game on TV.

"You know what, Dad, we don't need you," I told him.

And off my mother and I went. We sat in the middle of a mediocre restaurant. I had just come back from England, where I'd been researching a story about manners. I told her about the lunch I'd had at the Houses of Parliament, and the wedding I'd attended at which I felt naked because I wore a tux without tails. Then I explained what I'd learned about pouring milk into tea, how to butter a dinner roll, and how to hold a fork and knife in the English style.

"It's like this," I told her as I gently turned the fork in her frail hand. "That's it."

"I always wanted to learn to eat this way, but I never tried it until now," she said.

What I thought would be a dreary Mother's Day brunch—she was very sick at that point—turned out to be a delight for both of us. The way she listened always uplifted me. What greater gift could she give to an insecure and ego-maniacal writer than her delight?

And now I'm talking on and on about my Scotch trip and she is flailing and babbling in a hospital bed, unable to listen. She is like that the whole day, shifting, jagged, and unreachable.

The doctor doesn't know why she is agitated. My brother asks questions about what could be making her so uncomfortable. I watch him work the doctor as I've watched him work doctors for years, often with excellent results that push for answers and solutions. This time he gets nowhere. He is losing her and he knows it.

I feel for him.

The next morning, I return to her room, hoping to find her calmer, maybe even lucid. Instead, she is worse. The flailing is stronger, the lipstick now smeared on her teeth and face. I take a damp cloth, sit down, and wipe the red off the way she used to wipe the sand off me at the beach.

Hours later I wander out into the hallway to take a break. A nurse is standing at her station. She doesn't look busy. I step up and say hello.

"Can I ask a question about my mother, Mrs. Morris?" I say.

The nurse closes a folder. "Sure, what can I tell you?"

"She's been like this a while now, almost a week."

"I know, I'm so sorry."

"What is it? I mean, have you seen this kind of thing before?"

She takes a breath in, then lets it out and looks away. Her red hair is gray at the roots.

"To be honest, I only see this kind of thing at the end," she says softly.

"The end?"

"I mean when someone is at the end, there's a strange, desperate behavior like some kind of last long gasp for air, maybe like a kind of fight to hold on, or something like that. It's always the same. Nobody understands how someone so active could be so close to dying."

I let her words settle in. Then I look around, almost as if this conversation is illicit and I don't want to get caught. How to talk about something I've been thinking about for a while, always with bucketloads of guilt? I have seen my mother fall too often of late, cry out in pain when touched, and even soil herself in public, the most abject loss of control of all. Yet how can you not want someone you love and who loves you so much to go on living?

"So what do you recommend we do?" I ask.

A hospital visitor approaches with a question, then retreats. A phone rings. The nurse looks down to pick it up but changes her mind and looks right at me.

"I'd recommend you talk to her doctors about comfort care," she says.

"Comfort care?"

"Yes, palliative care."

"What is that?"

"It's more about easing pain than fighting for her life."

I never imagined that anyone in a hospital would articulate such a thing. Hospitals are all about treating illness and saving people, regardless of how compromised their lives are.

I thank the nurse and go to the men's room. I stare at myself in the mirror, wondering what kind of person I am. Am I able to advocate something that means giving up the fight? As I walk the corridor, white as cotton gauze, I start to steel myself for a conversation. Outside my mother's room, where my father naps in a chair, Jeff is conferring with two doctors.

I step up and introduce myself as the other son. The doctors, who have dealt with Jeff all week, greet me with skepticism and quickly turn back to him.

"Listen, I was just talking to the head nurse," I say.

They look at me. My heartbeat is quickening now. How do I say this?

"She told me that what's going on is something she sees when a patient is at the end."

The doctors, a man and a woman, go stock-still. Eventually, one nods, then the other.

"Is that something that makes sense to you?" I ask them.

The male doctor puts his arms around himself and his clipboard and nods, but almost imperceptibly, as if in shame.

The female doctor looks at him, then at my brother, then at me.

"Yes, it's very possible she's at that stage."

My brother's head shoots up. He looks at me and then asks her, "How do you know?" She looks at her colleague again. I feel an urge to step away but I hold my ground.

"We see it often, especially when there's a loss of brain function," she says softly.

I ask her what palliative care means. She explains it means removing all artificial life support and administrating a painkiller, morphine in this case, to alleviate all discomfort.

"As a side effect, it might hasten a peaceful ending," one doctor says.

We are quiet for a while, letting the gravity of the conversation have space.

"So if we agree, we could just make her comfortable and help her to the end," I say.

"But why?" Jeff asks me. "Because it's more convenient for you?"

Both doctors look away when they hear it. I look away too.

We say things in families, all kinds of them; some are forgotten later, some stay around longer. This question, this accusation with a searing truth in it, will stay with me for the rest of my life. I can't bear to see her suffer anymore. I'm tired of the worry and sadness. My father is too. And she needs help now to ease the anguish and the pain, that's clear.

So I don't refute my brother's accusation. I just step away and turn and walk down the hall and out the door.

Several hours later, after my father has agreed to our plan (it's not surprising, given his impatience with my mother and her infirmities all these years), Jeff and I are sitting on a bench in the tiny grassy area in front of the hospital. Traffic rushes farther uptown and then beyond to Connecticut, the Berkshires, and the Hudson River valley. It's a lonely August Friday in a city that empties out in late summer. Typically, Jeff and I would be gone too, he to his house in Westchester, me to my rental on Long Island. Not today.

Ten floors above us, my mother continues to rage and languish in her room. My father is taking a break and is back at their assisted living apartment. Jeff and I drink iced coffees, preparing ourselves for the longest eight hours of our lives. That's how long it can take, we've been told, once the morphine drip starts. It's three p.m. She could be gone by midnight.

"I still can't believe we might lose her so soon," Jeff sighs.

When he says that, what's left of my aggravation with him dissipates. He has already apologized for lashing out at me. Now he's doing the hardest thing, relinquishing the reins to let our mother, whom he loves fiercely, escape her suffering. There will be no more battles to find answers to unanswerable medical problems, the thrush in her mouth, the unstoppable growth of her spleen, the incontinence and imbalance, no more plugging holes in dikes against the flood tide of bodily breakdown. He's been doing this for so long and with such loving care that I can't imagine how he feels to think he may finally be stopping soon. I want to take his hand or put my arm around his shoulder. But that's not our way. We never hug or touch, unless it's to tease or tickle. He jumps if I even try. We are very close but not at all physical.

It's Friday, we realize. The Sabbath is coming: Shabbos, something our mother observed her whole life, calling us into the dining room, where she'd light the candles in her old brass candlesticks, heirlooms from her own parents, singing the blessings with a scarf on her head and waving her hands in circular motions to take in the flickering light as if it would bring her and all of us peace.

She loved all the Jewish holidays and often hosted the meals that brought cousins and friends to our table. Passover was a favorite, a complicated menu that took weeks to prepare. Even when she wasn't feeling her best, she'd labor at her brisket, kugel, and chicken soup. Nobody in the family, no aunt, cousin, or in-law, made matzoh balls better. They seemed as dense as her love.

The Seder was also the occasion for the mischief that only two silly and sarcastic sons could create. There wasn't a year when my brother and I didn't make each other laugh so hard that the grape juice would shoot from our noses. We got all the kids at the table laughing, rolling eyes at my father's bossiness as the "ritual head of the household," reclining as is the tradition (against a throw pillow) at the end of the table. If there were jokes to make at the responsive readings, we always found them. If there was a way to subvert the ritual of the afikomen—a game in which children hide a piece of matzoh—we would find it. And when it came time to welcome the Prophet Elijah into our home, a moment in which a child opens the front door to a spirit who we are told will join us at the table to drink wine from a glass set out for him, Jeff and I played a tape of ghoulish sound effects from under the table. Our guests would laugh, the kids especially. Our mother would not. She loved us but didn't understand why her own sons would turn something so sacred into something so silly. I don't know why now either. I loved those Seders, predictable as they were. We all did, year after year.

"You boys," she'd say as we helped her clean up.

"We're just having fun, Mom," I'd tell her.

I was the one to get blamed, the wicked son. On the other hand, nobody took the singing at those Seders more seriously than me. And while I'd take pride in knowing the tunes to so many blessings and prayers, and I would play the piano as we'd sing together after dessert, it was the pleasure she showed in all of us on those nights that made the holiday sacred. We teased her mercilessly as kids, and as I got further into adolescence, I'd pick fights with her too. But when I'd lead the singing with such command, there was no mistaking the pleasure in her eyes.

"We should get some candles," I say as we finish our iced coffees.

"It'll be her last Shabbos," Jeff replies as he throws his plastic cup away.

We're often in conflict, but I'm grateful to have such a caring man in my life.

She shows little sign of relaxing into the morphine drip several hours later. She is raging, as Dylan Thomas put it, against the dying of the light. And it worries all of us. My father, usually so optimistic, looks almost disgusted. I find it impossible to understand where she is getting the energy to keep thrashing.

"She doesn't want to go," Jeff says.

It pains me to think he believes that. But he might be right. None of us knows that she is ready to stop living. Religious as she is, she isn't what we'd call a spiritually evolved person. She has never showed any affinity for New Age culture, with its hopeful treatises about the upside of illness and aging. And here she is now, trapped in some kind of madness that doesn't allow her to have her last words or let us know she is hearing ours. I read somewhere that people only let go when they feel their loved ones are ready for their passing. But watching her struggle, it's hard not to think that she is resisting having to die. She doesn't seem to want to go, not at all.

Or is it that she somehow knows that Jeff is not really ready?

The sunset tonight is spectacular. The windows face west, and the pollution over New Jersey burnishes and upgrades the gold light, casting a glow across the river, over high-rise apartment buildings, and into the room. We raise the blinds. We light the Sabbath candles on the windowsill. We say the prayers, her prayers, hoping she'll join in. But she doesn't.

"Look at the candles, Mom," I tell her.

"Good Shabbos, Ethel," Dad whispers.

"Good Shabbos, Mom," Jeff says.

Much as we want her to see this last Sabbath and sunset, two things that always made her so happy, we can't get her to face the window. Her head bobs and she babbles, slower now, but still agitated as the morphine continues into her veins, drip by drip.

We look at the sunset for her. We look until the sky is dark and so is the room, with only the last of the candles flickering.

Hours pass. My father wonders, in a very soft voice, if we should sing to her.

I only have to think for a moment and then "You Are My Sunshine" comes out of my mouth. We capture the song's harmonies well, even Jeff, who isn't as musical as the rest of us. But when we attempt "Look for the Silver Lining," and I suddenly see her so vividly and so young, I have to stop singing or I'll fall apart. I take a breath, then another, then rejoin to finish the song.

When we are too tired to sing anymore, I put on a recording of "September Song," but when it gets to the part about the days dwindling down to *a precious few*, my father raises his hand, trembling from arthritis, and tells me to turn it off. "Too sad," he says. "Please, it's too sad."

My brother tries a different CD, Norah Jones, the big hit of the summer, full of sad lullabies. When she sings "Come Away with Me," it seems perfect. But moments later, when she sings "Don't Know Why," I have to hide tears again.

I feel as empty as a drum, I don't know why I didn't come...

I don't know why I didn't come sooner, but am so relieved to be here now. And I'm so grateful to my brother for getting me here in his own forceful way.

I keep wondering, as time passes, how long it will be until she gives up and stops fighting. Will it take all night and into morning? How long can a body that's so emaciated fend off the final sleep? Her breathing has slowed, but not enough to indicate she's in her very last hour. My father looks worried, my brother more, still not ready to see her go. The blue scarf rests on the pillow by her head, which still moves back and forth in negation, it seems, her lips moving as if she has something to say, perhaps "Help me" or "Please, I'm not ready yet."

I don't know. All I know is that when I come back from a long cigarette break outside with my brother, where we hardly say a word to each other, she is still struggling. She just won't quit. Inappropriate as it is, I find myself annoyed, pissed off that we have all been cheated of a good death for her, and that instead we remain trapped in this prolonged and devastating doubt.

I sit close, shut my eyes, not wanting to see her another minute, and before I can stop, I find myself muttering: "Are you going to die already?" It makes me turn red and hot-faced. Nobody has heard, and yet it feels like I yelled it across the room, across the span of her last ten years of illness. Why did I say that? I should never have said it.

Soon she is finally visibly fading. It's after midnight; the hallways outside are empty and her breathing has markedly slowed. And then, who knows exactly how much longer after that, it could be minutes or hours, but it finally happens—her breathing stops. We are all there to see it. Her face, that once-beautiful face that made the high school students she taught before she became a librarian call her Yum Yum and made my father so proud wherever they went, that face I know as well as my own, stops moving with mouth and eyes wide open, a body tense with fight and fear. She looks the opposite of at rest. It is a terrible death mask, giving us no resolution and denying us the peaceful final moment we hoped would come.

A nurse comes in and asks if we'd like her to shut Mom's eyes and mouth. We would.

We watch her raise her hands to the stony haggard face and gently shutter the blue eyes and then, with nothing more than a clamp of her hand, close the mouth from its frozen scream.

We sit for a moment together, feeling the shifting of the world, the geometry of our family tilting from four to three. It's enormous what happens in the instant of death. The Buddhists have a word for the transitional state when the spirit has left the body but hasn't settled into a new one yet. It's called Bardo, a critical moment that determines where a soul will be reincarnated. I wonder, though, if it isn't a critical moment not only for the dying but for the living too. Who are we about to become in the wake of the death of someone so important? How do we feel about our last hours, weeks, years with this person? What will our thoughts be like in the future—leaden with regret, heavy with sadness, or full of a persistent, uplifting delight?

But there's no time for these thoughts. We have the workings of daily life to think about, grounded in logistics. For my father and me, the event is over now; there's nothing more to see, and we start collecting our things from the hospital room. I don't want to look at my mother's face anymore, hard and immobile as granite. Her spirit has gone. It's time to move on, clear the room, sign the papers, get the death certificate, think about a funeral on Monday morning, and make all the calls to arrange it. But Jeff stays still in his chair, staring at her.

His world has just been diminished, and for him there is no relief because of her death, only anguish and the remorseful conviction he'll always have that she wasn't ready to go.

So he sits and stares. It is the ultimate act of allegiance, but for reasons I wish I could understand better, I start to resent him for it. Then I tell myself to stop. He loves her so much.

He keeps us from turning to go. He keeps us with her a few minutes more.

The next morning I wake up on the couch of my parents' apartment in the city. While we may be relieved that Mom is finally gone and not suffering anymore, the truth is we can't just relax, maybe just sleep all day until we are good and ready to wake up into a new life in which a core character is missing. We can't just sweep our arms across the bathroom and kitchen counters and dump her pill bottles into the wastebasket to clear some room for Dad's things and wipe out the memory of her suffering by putting up photos of her when she was young and beautiful. We'll have to find those later. Dad can't watch a ball game as he'd like, and I can't go back to my beach cottage on eastern Long Island. We have work to do. Jewish tradition doesn't allow a long time to pass between a death and a burial. The funeral will be on Monday, two days from now. That has already been arranged. So today Dad and I have calls to make to let people know about it. Most of them are older, without e-mail.

I have my list and he has his, and while I am brutally brief as I call around, sharing the news and deflecting any long conversations or questions that require detailed explanations, I can hear Dad getting tripped up in the process. He's working his cell phone in the next room, sitting on the side of the bed. I walk over, stand over him like a tough-ass manager, and give him the "wind it up" sign with my finger. Sometimes I even bark, "Dad, can I talk to you?" to get him off the phone. He wants to assure people that my mother's passing was for the best. He wants to let them know he's fine, and he also wants to know how *they're* doing. It's very hard for him. His default mode is chipper.

Of course, when you've never done what we're doing, it's all hard. What do we know? The three of us, Jeff, Dad, and me, decide that before the burial we want to have a more formal memorial service at our old family synagogue in Bay Shore, a long drive from the cemetery. And then, despite a conversation with the rabbi, who has indicated that speeches given by the immediate family aren't standard (although he says he's noticed that people are doing them more and more), we decide that each of us will speak. That means that although we're exhausted and in a state of shock from Mom's death, we have to pull ourselves together to write our speeches on the night before the funeral. How do you encapsulate the essence of a mother when you can hardly keep your eyes open? I finish mine and ask my father if he needs help with his.

"I'm fine," he says. "I'll just speak off the top of my head."

I know that's a terrible idea but cannot dissuade him. So the next day he goes up and stands at the podium with Jeff and me seated behind him on the imposing old altar of the Bay Shore Jewish Center. Dad rambles in such a pointless and hopeless way, lost in his random musings about my mother's sad medical history, that at a certain point, when he becomes overwrought, I step up and escort him away from the microphone. Jeff speaks next, recalling our mother's habits with wit and equanimity. The pews are not full, and there are barely enough people in them—less than a hundred in all—to make me feel this memorial service is worth the trouble. But more than Dad and me, it's what Jeff wants, as he wants to endow the Hebrew school in our mother's name and put both our parents' names under one of the synagogue's ten big stained-glass windows. I scan for familiar faces the way I did when I sang in the choir for our High Holiday services, when we sang haunting Hebrew melodies with as much conviction as adolescents could manage. Back then, in my early teens, death was the last thing on my mind. My mother seemed immortal. My father, whose family had been founders of our synagogue, and who had been president of this congregation, had black hair then, not white. He played tennis daily. He loved to dance and putter in his garden. Life seemed to have nothing but potential for us and a happy embarrassment of choices. Our parents worked hard so that they could give us everything.

It's my turn to speak now. I step up with my typed remarks. They are about my mother's love of simple beauty—sunsets, stars, blossoming trees. But I can hardly get past the first paragraph before my chin starts to tremble. I am seeing her innocent smile, hearing her vulnerable, high-pitched voice. My whole face twists, a seizure of sadness, and I erupt into such violent weeping that I can't get the words out. I should just apologize and stop. Instead, I blubber through. When I sit down, I only look up for a moment to see the stricken faces of so many people whom I've managed to alienate with my grief. It is a mistake, I realize too late, to think it's possible to speak with composure so soon after a death of someone so close.

It's raining at the cemetery, and the graveside service, where there is only one small plaque in the ground indicating our mother's presence—the large family stone with the words, written in Hebrew, of a Yiddish lullaby she sang will come later—feels rushed as people run to and from their cars. They converge at our house later in what doesn't seem as much like a shiva—the Jewish tradition of visiting the home of the mourning family each day for a week after a death—as an attack. Even if someone wants to comfort us with a story or observation about our mother that we've never heard before, we are too busy greeting guests and receiving flowers and offerings of casseroles to appreciate it. Instead we are facing, at this moment that is as large as any we've ever faced, housekeeping details and small talk.

"So where do you live in the city?" a friend of my parents whom I'd never met asks.

"What kind of writing do you do?" asks another.

I can barely respond. People must know that this isn't the time for small talk. They must know that they aren't just responsible for showing up to honor our mother but are also meant to talk about her so we can keep her alive a little longer. But they don't. And it hurts because time is passing and every minute since her death a few days ago, she is getting further from us. I stand with gray tie loosened and feet aching in black shoes in the den where my mother and I used to sit in the sun, and where she made my brother and me fabulous birthday parties at a long folding table for a dozen children in birthday hats. She wore big-skirted dresses in those days, pearls and heels, we know it from the home movies we love to watch. In a living room packed with guests, I look at the piano and see her, sitting next to me playing duets. In the dining room, she's at the end of the table next to her kitchen, where everything is cooking in a miraculous display of her will to preserve holiday traditions despite the fact that she never liked to cook. She is still here in this house. And all I want as I scoot around and answer the door and play tag team with my brother and his wife, making sure there's enough ice, sandwiches, plates, and napkins for our guests, is to hear people talk about her. For years I thought she'd be better off dead and that I would be able to get the happiness in my life back with her gone. Now I want her back. All I want to do now is talk about her. And even if there is a moment to actually do it, nobody seems to know how.

∞

Several months later, we are helping Dad pack up the house they lived in for half a century. He kept it while living with my mother in the assisted living place in the city. Now he's moving out for good to another assisted living place. But this one's in Great Neck, on Long Island, where he's more comfortable. My brother thinks the Danish Modern furniture will have great value and hires an estate company to assess it. We are given the name of a carting company that will bring a Dumpster instead of an auctioneer. I do not tell him, "I told you so." Instead we roll our eyes and laugh.

It's my job to toss things from my mother's closet and dresser. There isn't much to save for Janet, my brother's wife, a vintage coat here, a string of pearls there. But the sight of the clothes my mother wore for years brings her back to me in a rush, just like the dishes she used for her baking—her meat loaf, macaroni and cheese, and any number of artificially sweetened and chemically rich low-calorie desserts that my brother sometimes called Love Canal cooking.

I stand at her closet, wondering how I went from admiring everything about her as a child to teasing her about not keeping up with fashion. As an adult, I often mocked her taste and tried to get her to be someone she wasn't. Sometimes she'd take offense, especially in her last years, when she was tired of my nagging her to exercise and dress better. Often she'd just laugh me off. How did someone so sincere raise such a shallow son? Why did she love me so much?

∞

In March, six months after she's gone, but before she starts appearing in my dreams, we are on vacation on the west coast of Florida, my father, my brother, and his six-year-old son, Ian, who only knew our mother as unwell but loved her with a sensitivity that made us proud.

My father is off watching a basketball game in our hotel, and the three of us are biking without him on a lovely peninsula with the sun setting over the Gulf of Mexico, a show-stopping display. We get off our bikes and sit down on a bench to enjoy it. Pelicans drift above us and gulls call in shrill tones, with the gold and pink light from the sky painting their wings.

"Are you thinking about Grandma Ethel right now?" Ian asks.

My brother and I exchange looks, the kind we only have for these family moments.

"Why do you ask, Ian?" my brother replies.

"Because I know how much she loved sunsets and I know how much you miss her."

"That's so true," I say.

"We miss her very much," Jeff says.

"But think of it—it's going to just be so great when you guys see her again," he says.

"When we see her again?" I ask.

"Yeah, up in heaven," he says. "It'll almost be as great as

on the day you were born and you looked up at her face and saw her for the very first time."

The sun nears the horizon. We put our arms around him and sit together in silence, three sons waiting for the last light of the day to leave our world.

Dad

Exit Strategy

My father loves pills, whether prescription or over-the-counter. Red ones. Pink, blue, yellow, and white ones. Capsules of one color and those that have two, pretty as Easter eggs. The ones you push out of foil packs like candy dots, and the ones in safety-sealed bottles that sound like maracas when you shake them. Pills for allergies and pills for high cholesterol. Muscle relaxants. Beta-blockers. Blood thinners, stool softeners, and acid reducers. And then there is the kind of sleeping pill he chose from his beloved pharmaceutical cornucopia when he wanted to die one sunny summer Monday—Ambien, a little white sleeping pill no bigger than a Tic Tac.

My spouse, Ira, and I are on the way back to the city from a friend's house in Connecticut when I get the call from Janet, my sister-in-law. My father, she tells me in a shaky voice, is with my brother in the emergency room at the hospital near Great Neck. I pull over to a rest stop to talk to her but struggle to hear above the roar of I-95.

"He's asleep but stable," she says. "It's very upsetting."

She tells me my brother drove out from the city the minute he heard the news.

"And is he planning to stay with him all day?" I ask.

"Of course," she says. "I know he'd like you to be there too."

I thank her and hang up. The sun beats down and the interstate traffic rushes by as I think about what to do. I have a column due the following day. To get it done, it would be so much better to head to the hospital tomorrow, not today. How much am I needed? When I tell Ira the situation, he looks at me with something like scorn. "You have to go right now," he says.

Maybe I'm in denial. If I don't let this crisis change my plans for the week, will it be contained? My father's increasing fragility and shortness of breath have been plaguing him for months. My brother and I didn't pay enough attention to his plight, it suddenly seems.

We get back on the highway. I check my rearview mirror, scratch my sunburned nose. It has been a wonderful weekend with an elderly friend who has emphysema but is still kicking. We didn't give it a second thought when invited to her grand and shingled seaside home. For my own father, I've been more careful about jumping to spend time and offer my services.

The exits to Manhattan and Long Island are up ahead— a fork in the road, two paths that diverge. I don't know the ratio of guilt to love that tips my balance—or maybe some divine hand takes the steering wheel from me, forcing me to do the right thing. At any rate, I am veering left and merging with traffic to go to my family where I'm needed, and away from Manhattan and work.

"Dammit," I mutter.

"So how did he do it?" asks Ira, a fun-loving book agent who enjoys my father's many quirks.

"He took six Ambien."

"How do they know it was a suicide attempt?"

"He left a letter."

"Only six Ambien?"

"What do you mean, *only* six Ambien?"

"That's about what I take when I get to Europe for a conference and need a good night's sleep."

We look at each other. I have to smile.

When I arrive at the hospital on Long Island, after dropping Ira off at a train to the city, my father is asleep in the emergency room and looking only a little ashen for a man who has taken what he thought was a dose to help him sleep forever. My brother gets up to give me his chair. He looks relieved that I've come right away.

"Look," Jeff says in something like a hopeful whisper. "It's Bob."

There isn't room for two visitors. So he steps away to leave us alone. Like a tortoise coming out from the mud to get some sun after a long winter, my father leans forward and opens his eyes, which are hazel, a color we share. His gaze catches mine and holds it a long time.

"Bobby," he finally sighs. Then his head falls back to his pillow.

My eyes fill with tears. "Hi, Dad. I'm here," I whisper.

I take his soft, arthritic hand, which I know as well as my own. His wrist is connected to an IV port. Over the emergency room noise—the voices and beeping of machines—he resumes snoring. Now that I'm here and see him hooked up to all the tubes and wires, it strikes me harder: he wanted to die and we had no idea that his desperation about his failing health had become so intense. "Do you think he'll be asleep for a while?" I ask a nurse checking his signs.

"He's still groggy," she says. "He'll wake up soon."

"And he'll be okay?"

"Oh, yeah," she says with a trace of a grin. "You can take a whole bottle of Ambien and it won't kill you. It just isn't that kind of drug."

"That's a relief," I say.

"And he took—how many? Five or six? That's nothing."

"It's probably all he had handy. He doesn't always think things through."

"Well, you're lucky. If he'd taken something else, he'd be gone."

I detect a kind of cynical empathy in her voice, if such a thing is possible. Perhaps she is acknowledging what I can't get out of my thoughts. This fiercely independent eighty-two-year-old man, who still drives and really doesn't want to be a bother, has just brought a great deal of bother on himself and his family. What are we going to do with him now? How many more years will he live against his will after his suicide has failed? Suicide with six pills? What was he thinking? Well, he's careless, I know it, and like me, he often takes half-assed measures. He's also impulsive, and he makes plans that tend to complicate rather than simplify. His logic has always been as sloppy as his eating habits. And everywhere he goes he leaves piles of papers—newsletters, coupons, and throwaway newspapers. In his car he still has a hundred tennis balls from the days when he played, a dozen yarmulkes, bridge columns, visors, pairs of sneakers, books, old X-rays, brochures for time-shares that he'll never buy, underwear, socks, and half-eaten sandwiches. And between the driver's and the passenger's seat, he keeps an old Styrofoam cup of his beloved pills. Mostly they're for allergies, which hit him in spring just as they do me. Anytime I would sneeze in his car, he would stick his hand in that cup and pull something out for me.

"Dad, those are prescription," I'd always tell him. "Stop forcing them on me!"

"Some are over-the-counter, but suit yourself—just trying to help," he'd say.

Looking at him in his emergency room bed, I think about all the times I said no to his pills, and the look of disappointment that darkened his face. Then I think about the times I said no to all his other requests. He wanted to rent a vacation place with me last summer. He wanted to show me all his bank statements to let me see the money I would inherit.

"Why, Dad? Are you planning to die soon?" I asked last week at his kitchen table.

"No, but I want you to see what your mother and I saved for you."

"I don't want to know," I said. "Forget about it."

Maybe I should have said yes. Maybe it would have helped him feel more powerful when he was suffering from the erratic heart that made him feel so weak and fragile.

I wonder, *Is there a pill a son can take to open his heart to his father?*

Machines buzz and click. Beyond our curtains, patients are coming and going, some on foot, some on gurneys. It's not the best place to sit and ruminate over my treatment of a good-hearted dad who's always been my biggest fan. Nor is it a happy place for him to wake and face the fact that he will be doomed to live. I go outside to sit at the hospital's front entrance, busy with cabs and cars, joining my brother. He's on his phone, so I call Doreen, Dad's long-distance girl-friend, who was visiting from Florida when she found him on the floor this morning.

"Oh, Bobby," she sighs. "How are you?"

"Shocked, but I guess I shouldn't be that surprised."

"Of course you should be surprised. I had no idea he was so down."

I want to ask her why not. But I know the answer. It's

because she is his joy and he would never let on to her that he feels threatened by the health of his heart. Doreen is the lively woman my father started dating a year after my mother died. Their romance made him happier than he'd been in years, and he deserved some fun after being with an ailing wife for so long. He'd only been living it up with Doreen for a year when his heart and energy faltered. Their fun slowed. And because they never moved in together, my brother and I don't know what to expect of her now. If I were in her shoes, I'd be halfway out the door. Suicide? People face all kinds of problems in life, but few are so troubling.

"I'm sorry you got dragged into this, Doreen," I tell her.

"It's not your fault," she says. "We all do the best we can."

"Do you need anything?"

"No, just some rest," she says. "Call me when there's news."

I say I will and hang up. My brother's still on an office call. I notice a man with his wheelchair-bound father on the next bench. The son, in a crisp poplin suit and Hollywood sunglasses, has deals spinning, I can tell, and he speaks percussively into his phone. Even in the flattering golden light of a late-summer afternoon (birds all around making a racket), the old father looks pale under a Mets cap. He's trying to whistle and can barely get a sound out.

He could be our father. Will this be the next ten years for us?

When Jeff gets off the phone, he tells me that Dad attempted his suicide while Doreen was leaving for Vermont this morning. They had rented a cheap condo on a ski mountain for August. When he told her yesterday that he didn't feel well and encouraged her to go alone, she didn't refuse. Soon after, he went into the bathroom to take his life.

"Here's the letter," Jeff says.

From his briefcase he pulls out some pieces of yellow legal paper. He holds them out to me. Dad's scrawl is more legible than it has ever been. The letters are big, bold, and uppercase.

To Doreen and Family:
I hope you'll forgive me for leaving you. I love you all so much. But I just can't handle being so helpless.

The rest of it, which goes on for three pages, is about practicalities—how much to tip staff people in the dining room of his assisted living facility; where to find his will; who will get his furniture, TV, and car. He has also left a long biography. I feel a lump form in my throat as I read it. He wants so much to be acknowledged. But ultimately, although he's a memorable character with a lovely singing voice and a great affinity for puns and parodies, he hasn't done much. He wants an obituary to trumpet his accomplishments—zoning laws he put into place on Fire Island; offices he held at the Suffolk County Republican Club, the family synagogue, and our Cub Scout troop; also his certification as an umpire for the Eastern Lawn Tennis Association. I have to smile when I read where he wants his obituary published—several Long Island newspapers right away and more in Florida, but months from now in the winter, "in season," he writes, when his snowbird pals will be down there. It strikes a chord, given my own struggles for recognition. But it's a strange way to say good-bye. His letter has little emotional content for a man who can be so sweet and sentimental. It's mostly a list of instructions.

"But he thought everything through," Jeff says.

"Except his method."

"Maybe it was more a gesture, a cry for attention."

"Yes, maybe," I sigh, feeling my shoulders tighten. "Well, if he wanted our attention, he's got it now."

For months we've been ignoring his quiet despair about his failing heart.

"You'll continue to feel weaker and weaker," his cardiologist told him in May, "and although this is hard to accept, there's really nothing you can do about it."

Now, I don't know what the medical code of ethics says about truth-telling versus soft-pedaling. But might this doctor have been a little less direct? Could he have suggested a course of physical therapy or nutrition (Squeeze a rubber ball every morning! Eat lots of smoked salmon with omega oils! Do yoga!), if only for the feeling of control it might have instilled? Why say it's over? My father's a man, after all, who lives on hope, shuffling along in his beige vinyl loafers and margarine-yellow cardigan with a song in his heart and half-price coupons in his wallet for an early-bird dinner. Up until recently, he always assumed things would work out. When his shortness of breath first started, he thought he'd found a cure in chocolate.

"It makes me feel a hundred percent better," he kept telling me last winter.

But all the chocolate in the world can't fix a failing heart.

When my brother and I go back to the emergency area, we find that our father has been moved to a regular hospital room upstairs. He's lying awake over white sheets in a pale blue gown. His smudged aviator glasses sit crooked on his nose. We didn't expect to see him awake so soon and haven't had a chance to collect our thoughts. What do you say to someone who has just woken up to find that, against all his wishes, he's still alive? *Welcome back?*

"You're awake," I chirp.

"Hi, Dad," Jeff follows.

"Nice to see you guys," Dad says.

Jeff and I exchange looks. *Nice to see you guys?* He always loves our visits and is gracious enough to tell us so. But what to say now about what he has done to himself? A family more in touch with feelings, a more open and therapized one, that is, would talk about it. Instead, we go into planning mode. And the first thing on the agenda, our father tells us, is a visit from the hospital's psychiatrist. A moment later, a pale, middle-aged man with a ponytail, a blue blazer, and black clogs walks in: Dr. Jack Downer. The irony of the name makes my brother and me raise eyebrows. Dr. Downer gets right to work. Like someone taking a survey, he asks my father the basics—if he knows the day and if he can count backward by sevens. My father, a lover of crossword puzzles and sudokus, scores well and enjoys the attention. His mood, verging on buoyant, as if nothing has happened today, is inappropriate at best.

"Have you ever had psychiatric problems, Mr. Morris?" Dr. Downer asks.

"No! Never! And I've never been to a therapist either."

"Did you really intend to die?"

Jeff and I cringe at the question.

"Yes, and I actually chose a Monday to do it because I figured it would be more convenient for my boys and not disturb their weekend plans."

"I see," the doctor says.

I wish that Dr. Downer weren't quite so true to his name and could be a little more uplifting. He doesn't sit, but rather stands as far from the bed as possible. Is he being intentionally distant while judging my father for being weak and foolish? Are we?

"Had you been very depressed?" he asks.

"It got worse and worse as I realized I couldn't do the things I liked to do."

"When you woke up from the attempt a while ago, were you glad to be alive?"

My father doesn't say anything. He pushes white strands of hair from his head and we wait for his response. Outside in the hall, a noisy family shuffles past with a doctor escorting them to the elevator, worried looks on their faces. This is what he so wanted to avoid, a prolonged ending on a low note. If I were in his position, I might have tried the same thing. I'm all for the simple solution, the easy exit. Ira calls me a plug-puller and jokes that I will not be in charge when he's at the end. He's not wrong. He knows how I lobbied to send my mother off as quickly as possible. And I ponder calling it quits for myself all the time too. Terminal illness? Spare me the surgery and show me the door. Why must the show go on?

"I was prepared to live," my father finally answers. "I wasn't sure the pills would work." I sigh. The doctor makes a note. Then he tells my father he will have to be moved to a locked psychiatric ward for observation tomorrow. It's the law in New York State.

"By technical standards, you are a danger to yourself, Mr. Morris," he says.

My father, a man more comfortable facing open heart surgery than any thoughts of his own dark and uncontrollable subconscious, winces. He might be wacky, but he's not crazy, and suddenly I feel another jab of pain for him and squirm about his predicament.

"I'd really appreciate it, Doc, if I could spend the night in this bed and then just go home in the morning and forget this whole thing," he says.

"I don't think that's possible," Dr. Downer says with detachment.

"Why not? I made a mistake, and I won't do it again."

"But do you still want to die, Mr. Morris?"

My father looks over at me and then at my brother. We lean in toward him from our chairs, helpless. It feels as if the entire hospital has gone silent. We wait for his answer.

"No, but I still would like to put an end to being dependent on others so much," he says.

Dr. Downer leans against a ledge and softens his tone. Behind him, Pepto-Bismol-pink sky illuminates a window and his long, bristly hair.

"Aren't there things you do that you can enjoy on your own, like reading or cards?" he asks.

"Not really. Look, to be honest, I'm out of plans."

"Well, that's not very reassuring, Mr. Morris."

"But I know I've had a wonderful life," my father adds. "And when I woke up just now to see my boys here, it made me see how much they love me. So that's a positive thing."

"Yes, it's good that you can see that your sons love you."

A pleading tone comes into my father's voice as I stand over him as if to protect him.

"Just let me go home tomorrow, Doc. I'd really like to forget about this whole affair."

"Unfortunately, suicide survivors don't always get a say, Mr. Morris."

My father sighs. I feel frustrated for him, knowing he's trapped and that he will have to pay for the mistake of not finishing himself off properly, which turns out to be common with the suicidal. They don't drown as they'd intended, or they throw up the pills they take. Or someone finds them just in the nick of time, and by saving them ruins their careful exit strategy.

Outside, the sun is turning from pink to borscht red. Carts of hospital dinners roll by in a feeding-time rush hour. The interview is winding down. But Dad, desperate to keep playing the host and keep the conversation going, wants to be reminded of his interrogator's name.

"It's Dr. Jack Downer, Mr. Morris," the doctor says.

"So is there a Jill for you, Jack?" my father, the habitual matchmaker, asks.

"What do you mean?"

"You know—so that a Jack and a Jill can go up the hill to fetch a pail of water?"

The doctor looks at his clogs. My brother turns red. I smile, then keep my smile from widening, as I often have to around such an uncontrollable well-meaning yenta of a father.

"No, there isn't," says the doctor with his head now cocked to one side. "Why?"

"Because I'm going to fix you up," my father says. "That's what I like to do."

The doctor steps forward to stare like an ornithologist inspecting a rare species of bird. My brother and I look away to hide our laughter. The father we find so amusing and embarrassing has returned to us for a moment, and we are overjoyed to see him.

"That's a funny thing to suggest to a doctor you just met,"
Dr. Downer says. Then, after a long pause, something like the
trace of a smile crosses his pale, narrow face. "But I'm open
to it."

"Doc," my father says, "you just gave me a very good
reason to live."

Once home, he forgets his promise. And he takes no pleasure in resuming his life. I can't get him to leave his apartment when I visit. Why must he wallow in his decrepitude?

"He wants to show us he was right to kill himself," my
brother tells me.

"What's to keep him from trying again?" I ask.

One day in July I am coaching him before seeing the
house doctor in his assisted living building. This is the man
who can write an antidepressant prescription. "Now, Dad," I
say as I watch him struggle to pull on his socks. "Don't turn
on the charm for this doctor or he might not prescribe anything. You need to show him how miserable you are. Don't
talk too much, okay?"

"Don't worry, Bobby," he says. "I'll show him a terrible
time."

Well, not exactly. He uses the overbooked doctor's minutes in a cramped office with a line of patients outside to brag
about me and then tell the story of his own life, with the
sadness of being an orphan deleted. I listen to him with foot

tapping. He talks about his stint performing skits in the army and his career as an administrative law judge at the New York Department of Motor Vehicles. He talks about his beloved tennis, bridge, and wife. In that order.

"She was beautiful—wholesome like Anne Baxter," he says of my mother.

"What about your depression, Dad?" I coax.

"Yes, is there any depression in your family?" the doctor asks.

"Not really," my father says.

"Any dementia?"

"Try me. Or tell me a joke and I'll tell you if it's funny."

I shoot him a look and gesture to tone it down.

"I'm just going to take your blood pressure instead," the doctor says. "And I'm prescribing Zoloft."

"Sounds good," Dad says. "I'll be happy to give it a try. Or unhappy, I mean."

My heart is pounding as the doctor writes the prescription, which I hope is a strong one. We leave his office, and while my father goes upstairs, I run so fast to the drugstore that I almost get hit by a car. I am desperate for the Zoloft to work so that he will go back to enjoying his life, so that I can go back to enjoying mine. I don't want to take emotional care of him. I want the Zoloft to do the work instead. It's ironic. His whole life, I mocked his belief in the power of allergy pills, muscle relaxants, beta-blockers, and diuretics. Now I hold a prescription for him as if it's something between a boarding pass and a winning lottery ticket. I want to believe that a medication can transport him and all of us away from the overpowering undertow of his sadness.

In the months after the suicide attempt, singing is our default activity. But even with the Zoloft, Dad's in a deep well of depression. So I get him out of his apartment and down to the lobby of his building, away from his gloomy full-time health aide, Bea, who has to be living with him for legal reasons—neither the management of the building nor the state government trusts that he won't try to kill himself again. I come out from the city with work problems on my mind, in particular about a solo show I'm to perform soon. Ironically, it's about him and his wacky and wonderful year of trying to find love after my mother died. The love he found, Doreen, is back in Florida—no help to us. In his lobby, I sit at a grand piano with a plastic flower arrangement.

He sits on the striped chintz couch and I, armed with books of show tunes, sight-read my way through dozens of songs. When I can't quite wrap my fingers around the complex chords and key signatures of melodies by Gershwin, Berlin, and others, we sing through anyway. "Always," "I'll Be Seeing You," "Where or When," "Till There Was You." The lyrics of these songs become almost metaphysical to me. They have such wisdom and passion.

Some things that happen for the first time
Seem to be happening again

Dad's nostrils flare and the flecks of gold in his eyes reflect the light as he strains to hit the notes. Often we harmonize, sometimes like howling dogs, other times precise as professionals. We sing as residents walk past, mostly ignoring us. Some sit down and sing along. It makes me swell with delight. Whenever I see people having tough times with aging parents, I tell them to try to find what they like to do and do it together. Whether it's looking at old photos, playing Scrabble, watching classic movies, or shopping, what matters is finding some pleasure in the time. Too bad my dad won't humor me about finding him a new match.

Each time a remotely attractive woman passes by, I try to get him to engage. (I'm as much the yenta as he is.) He never rallies, not even for Ronna, a svelte blonde with good jewelry. "You should have a real date with her," I say one afternoon. "Ask her out."

"Bobby, please don't be stupid," he says with a wave of his hand.

"You need to meet someone."

"I already told you those days are over for me."

"You know how women inspire you."

"But I already have Doreen."

"But she's not here for you! She lives in Florida!"

I close the music book at the piano and sit down on the couch next to him. I'm more frustrated than I have a right to be, I know. It's his life, not mine. His nails are dirtier than usual, his plaid button-down soiled. People are waddling and wheeling past to dinner as the elevator dings and dongs. So many of them are worse off than he is—they have less mobility, money problems, and children who have abandoned them or only visit rarely. How do they manage to look so cheerful? How do they go on in such compromised circumstances?

"You need some romance, old man," I say.

He grunts and, with some effort, forces himself up off the couch.

"Don't push me, Bobby, I'm warning you."

One day, when I'm visiting him with Ira, I move in on an attractive woman reading the *Times* in his lobby. She's a handsome ash blonde named Honey whom I've been scoping for weeks.

"This may sound strange," I tell her. "But would you like to join us for lunch?"

She looks me up and down, thinks a moment, then says, "Why not?"

Moments later, I'm at the wheel of Dad's car with Ira beside me. In the back, my father sits with Honey. He won't talk to her. "So, Honey, how long have you lived in the building?" I ask.

"Two years November," she says in what seems a patrician accent.

"Have you two seen each other around before?"

"Of course," Honey says. "Everyone knows Joe."

I check the rearview mirror. A Joe that fewer people know is staring out the window, grimacing and refusing to look at us. It's as if all his natural affability and amiability have been drained from his body. I have to fight the urge to demand that he join the conversation.

On East Shore Drive, we pick up Ira's mother, Lillian. She jumps into the back in one of her fly girl hats—white and kind of gangster rapper. Superfly. "L'il Lil," I call her. She's eighty-three years old, a little older than my father, and full of life, good cheer, and liberal politics.

"Thanks for joining us, Ma," Ira tells her.

"Of course," she says. "I love being with you guys."

Ira and I look at each other. He takes my hand. I feel a rush of well-being. Something about the scenario is making me happy, despite my father. I like myself for making an effort, first of all, but what I like even more is having Ira here with me. After being single or in doomed relationships my whole adult life, I am finally settling in with a vital and stylish man who makes me feel more alive than I've felt since college. The moment I introduced them two years ago, he and my father were talking as if they'd known each other forever. That's why it's so disconcerting to see Ira unable to engage him now.

"Joe," he says. "What's got your interest in the news these days?"

"Not too much," my father sighs.

"Any thoughts on the 2008 election yet?"

"Not really."

I look in the rearview mirror again. Lil and Honey are chatting away. Dad stares out.

We find a great place for lunch on the water in Port Washington. It's a sunny late-July Saturday, and from our table on the porch the harbor glistens, and everyone is engaged in conversation but my father. My resentment is growing. I mutter to Ira that I've had it with him.

"Why aren't the antidepressants working?" I ask.

"They take time," he says. "Give your old man a break."

When Dad asks me to help him to the bathroom, I wait for him outside his toilet stall as if he were prey. He comes out to wash his hands. I pounce. "You really should be making more of an effort," I say.

"This is the best I can do for now," he says.

"Dad, you're on Zoloft, why aren't you cheering up?"

"You think it's that simple?"

He holds his hands under a dryer and I yell over the noise.

"Look, you're making all of us miserable. I need you to buck up."

No answer. He keeps drying. I am now screaming.

"Who do you think you are, dragging us all into your misery? You have a good life, we all love you so much, so why can't you do us all a favor and fucking buck up?"

The dryer shuts off. The silence hits me like a punch in the gut.

"If you can't handle it, don't come around anymore," he says.

I turn and leave him there. My pulse races as if I've just committed a crime.

In late August, he tries to sabotage an appointment with a psychologist that my brother has gone to great trouble to arrange. *August*, when every shrink is on vacation. Dr. Kahn even takes Dad's insurance. On a not-unpleasant Tuesday afternoon I park on a pretty Great Neck street that is only a half block from the entrance of a small, brick medical building.

But Dad isn't getting out of the car. He sits still in the passenger seat.

"Come on, Dad, we don't want to be late."

I open his door and lean down to give him a hand to pull him up.

"I'm not feeling up to walking right now," he says.

This is his latest, the refusal of any form of exercise.

"Oh, come on, just a few steps. Nothing to it."

It's a beautiful day, with lovely shade trees lining the street of aging mock-Tudor buildings. I give him both hands and pull him up and help him steady himself at the curb.

"Okay," I say like a personal trainer. "The entrance is right there—ready?"

He takes a step in his blue canvas deck shoes, wobbly and tentative as a toddler. Then he takes another two or three steps before stopping.

"Come on, Dad, let's go!" I chirp.

"Please don't push me," he says in a raspy tone.

"I'm only pushing you because we're late."

"I'm having a hard time."

"You can do this, Dad. You want me to help?"

"You can help by not pushing me."

I'm moving from irritated into the zone of pissed. How dare he not make an effort to get to this appointment, which has taken weeks of research to secure? And who does he think he is, giving up on walking? My brother and I are both becoming afraid that if he doesn't walk he will lose his muscle tone and end up in a wheelchair. A wheelchair would be a whole new level of problematic. A parent in a wheelchair means added difficulties and inconveniences.

"Okay, let's move it, Dad," I bark.

He snarls but obeys, taking seven or eight steps, halfway to the entrance, before leaning back against a towering oak to catch his breath.

"I'm too winded," he says.

I don't believe him. I think he's just lazy and faking, even when I know he has a serious heart condition. While he has never liked walking, I have more faith in it than in God. Exercise is my answer to everything, and when I can't make him move I grow frustrated. I pushed exercise on my mother too, nagging her to take walks even when she was too weak to make it out the door. If only I had known that her lungs were damaged from her blood disease. But we didn't find that out until her last days, after years of her enduring my nagging to take walks with me. I would never have pushed so hard. She didn't need it. Neither does my father.

Dad is fighting each step to his appointment. I wonder if the idea of seeing a psychiatrist to talk about his despair is so alienating to him that he will do anything to avoid it. How can a visit to a doctor, he may be wondering, help with the fact that he can't enjoy life anymore?

"Let's go, Dad, almost there—we've got two minutes before you're late."

"I can't make it."

"Yes, you can."

"Don't you see those steps, Bobby?" His voice is a bleat.

"It's like six steps, there's a railing! I'll help you!"

"Why don't you call the doctor and ask if he'll come down and see me?"

"Here? On the street?"

"No. In my car."

The clock is ticking. His session is going to go to waste. I call upstairs.

"Dr. Kahn, you have an appointment with Joseph Morris, and I'm his son."

"Yes?"

"If you look outside your window you can see us."

I look up to see a silver-haired man in wire-rimmed glasses—someone who could be a relative—looking down from his second-story office. I wave. He nods.

"I have a kind of strange request. Can you meet with my father outside?"

There's a long Freudian pause. Or perhaps Jungian. Then, "Excuse me?"

"He's refusing to walk up your front steps."

"The building is wheelchair accessible, there's a ramp in the back."

"So you can't come down?"

"Sorry, that's just not possible."

Of course it isn't. So my only option is to get Dad a wheelchair. I call Bea, his sluggish aide, and ask her to run one over—we're only a few blocks from his apartment. We wait, him against the tree, me on the sidewalk, checking my watch and messages. Do I have time for this nonsense? His appointment will be very short now, a half hour at the most.

Wasted therapy! Squandered answers! I am seething.

"Keep this up, Dad, and you'll be in a wheelchair full time," I say.

"Don't say that to me."

"Then why can't you make an effort?"

Now a plangent whine, something like an off-key oboe, comes out of his mouth.

"Please, *please* don't nag me. I know you have good intentions, but you're making this very hard. If you keep it up, I'd rather you just stay away. What I need now is your support."

I think how nice it would be to stay away. But I actually can't imagine it. Much as he is driving me crazy, keeping away is not an option. He is suffering.

"If I don't make you try, you're going to lose all capability," I bark.

"You have to let me do things the way I want. I'm not a child, Bobby."

I know he's right. I don't want to make him more miserable. I guess I'm thinking that tough love might rouse him, along with therapy and more antidepressants. Clearly, seeing him with any woman other than the absent Doreen is no longer a possibility. I know that now. Finally, from around the corner, Bea appears, rushing along with a wheelchair. She is sweating from the exertion and looking, as usual, both bemused and skeptical at our father-son routine.

"Thank God," I say.

We put my dad into the chair and I wheel him to the building and up its ramp.

A few minutes later we sit in a tasteful office with a Chagall print on the wall. Given the chaos he has just caused, my father looks surprisingly together for his abbreviated psychotherapeutic encounter. The classic fifty-minute session has become the Joe Morris In-N-Out Burger of far less time. I am flustered but still hoping for some quick and easy insight.

"I've always believed an elderly person has the right to die, to decide what to do," my father declares in a sober voice I imagine he used when he worked as a motor vehicle judge.

"Well," says Dr. Kahn, who has a gentle, nonjudgmental demeanor that is the opposite of mine. "That's certainly a philosophical position."

"If I lived in Oregon, I would be able to legally choose for myself," Dad adds.

"It's not quite that simple—there are still procedures for getting approval from experts," Dr. Kahn says. "But look, I know this time of life isn't easy."

"You can say that again."

"Your wife died, there's been grief."

I think, *I guess so. But he certainly got back on the horse to get a girlfriend the moment she passed away—it was faster than you could type "find and replace."*

"Maybe you have some guilt around the death of your wife?" Dr. Kahn continues.

I think, *Maybe a little, but not that much.* I'm the one with the guilt, and I still question myself for not being there enough for her and not being sympathetic enough.

"But you're also in a new stage in your life, and you can't do the things you're used to doing," Dr. Kahn continues. "It requires that you reflect and find some meaning."

"Meaning?" my father says. "I have no regrets about my life."

"But the issue now is how do you cope and adapt? You have an unalterable illness."

"That's why I don't want to live."

"But you are alive, Mr. Morris. It's just that now you're at a new stage in life where the horizons are no longer infinite and things are looking very different."

"The Zoloft I'm taking is helping a little, but not enough."

"It may take some time. But it's also up to you. Are you

able to imagine accepting your circumstances so you can live your life in a way you find enjoyable?"

My father sighs, then he's quiet for a while. I can see his forehead furrow. He doesn't really want to get into a long discussion about his mortality or anything that might be too deep.

"All I want is to be as comfortable as I can be right now," he says.

"I'd like to help," Dr. Kahn replies.

Time is up. We make another appointment. I had hoped for more insight from this first visit, some life-changing silver-bullet observation to pull Dad back from his abyss. That might come over the course of many sessions, but clearly not in one day.

But my father refuses to see Dr. Kahn again.

"He's not willing to work on himself," I tell Ira.

"Is that a surprise?" he asks. "None of you Morris men are."

We are up at the house we recently bought in the mountains. It is a miracle to me, the first home I ever owned, and I own it with someone I love—a modest little farmhouse in a modest little village. But it is impeccably renovated and has a view of the mountains that makes us grateful. The only problem is the neighbors are a little too close and the river has turned chocolate-milk brown after a season of flooding. It drives me crazy that it doesn't look pristine.

"Rivers aren't this color in Connecticut," I fume.

"Nothing you can do about it," Ira says. "You have to learn to be more accepting."

He's right. And there's nothing I can do about my father either, I realize as I stare from a bridge over our roaring brown river taking its downward course to the sea. It is what it is. So is life. The only thing I can do now for my father is be there for him with all the love I can find.

All through the fall, I take him on drives around Long Island's Gold Coast—scenic and historic—and it's a much more pleasant way to pass a day than sitting in his cramped apartment. It's something to enjoy *together*, just as I did with him and my mother for so many years before. Like singing, driving to nice places feels more like pleasure than obligation. We play his old music in the car. Loquacious as he's been his whole life, a man who talks to anyone, he doesn't say all that much. When he does speak, it's often to hound me to find him a lethal dose of pills. Perhaps some sons would respond to that harshly. But I want him to know that I understand his interest in a final exit. I have seen a documentary about assisted suicide in which a son who helped his father die said he couldn't imagine not telling him *Yes, Dad, you can die at home, and yes, I'll help you get the pills and I will be with you on your last day.*

I tell Dad I'll do some research and report back. He has already been reading up on the "death with dignity" movement and has been talking to me about how great it is that more and more countries are allowing people to choose to die when they're ready. It's not that simple, and here, in the few states where assisted suicide is legal, a doctor has to deem you sufficiently incapacitated and in pain to write a prescription for a lethal dose of "medication" that you can take at home, rather than being given it in a hospital the way my mother was, as comfort or palliative care. But those "medications" taken at home don't always work. And then sometimes the person who is there to hold your hand and make sure everything goes smoothly gets busted by angry relatives and even arrested for murder, and has to go to court and suffer a dramatic, prolonged trial.

It's daunting, but Dad is so desperate that I can't resist looking into how I could help him out. I don't have access to pills. Suffocation with a pillow to his face seems too violent. Many user-friendly websites from various organizations suggest that the best exit—clean and efficient—is with a "helium hood." You place a plastic bag over the head and run a tube from a party balloon helium tank inside, then rubber-band it securely around the neck. Very quickly, the person will be getting no oxygen and will black out. Within twenty minutes, it's over. The only hitch is that people reach to remove the hood when they panic for oxygen. That's why it's best to have a helper at the bedside. And then, once the heart stops, it's recommended by organizations such as the Final Exit Network that the "guide" wait an hour before calling for an ambulance. The heart is a strong muscle, and emergency medical technicians can show up and restart it with relative ease, leaving someone alive but with weakened brain function.

It's a delicate art, helping death along. But the hood is a more foolproof method than pills because unlike in the days of the barbiturates that Marilyn Monroe took, most sleeping pills now (like Ambien) are not lethal. Also, if you don't have antinausea pills in the mix, you can throw everything up. Asphyxiating yourself in the car in the garage? Again, not recommended due to carbon monoxide filtering by the catalytic converters now required on all engines. Other methods—the messy and inconsiderate options of guns and nooses, for instance—are disparaged on various assisted suicide sites. All the online information keeps leading to the helium hood and then to ads for "kits" for sale from businesses flying in the face of the law and anyone appalled by the idea of euthanasia.

Dire as it all is, I have to laugh when reading the instructions: You must remember that if you're using a helium hood and you want to speak any last words to the universe or to the person seeing you out, those words will come out sounding like Daffy Duck. Helium makes the voice higher.

Of course, I don't tell my father about this. All I can do is bargain with him to live another month or so, give us a little more time as the weeks go on and the weather on Long Island turns from mild to cool. My niece's—his

granddaughter's—big-deal Bat Mitzvah will be in November. A suicide before then, or even a natural death, is out of
the question. It will ruin everything for my brother and his
family. So I tell Dad it would be rude not to stick around.
He agrees, but without enthusiasm for the upcoming festive
occasion. Time for him is now just a burden. For me it has
become a bargaining chip. I've become the gatekeeper of his
mortality.

"You have to wait," I say.

He's in a better mood than usual on a pleasant October
afternoon as I steer his car past the boxy mansions of Great
Neck. Bea, the sullen and sedentary Jamaican aide, is in the
backseat, surrounded by his junk. She is not listening to her
iPod today.

"You're upbeat," I tell him. "What's that about?"

"I'm feeling pretty good right now," he replies. He is
wearing clean clothes for once, something I assume is due to
Bea's keeping an eye on him. He looks smooth, cute.

"Great to hear it, Dad. May I be so bold as to ask why?"

His answer shoots out of him with more bravado than
I've heard in months.

"Because Doreen was just here and we had a lovely
weekend."

His voice has that old mellifluous crooner's tone I love.
The energy I've been hoping for is finding its way back to us
today, and my voice trembles with pleasure.

"She came up to see you? I didn't know that!"

"It was her grandson's birthday in Jersey, but she came to see me afterward."

"No wonder I haven't heard from you in days! What did you do?"

"We played bridge with my friends, went out to dinner and a movie, just like we did all last winter in Florida. We had a ball and I feel better than I have in months."

"So you're still a hot item, then?"

"Never any question."

"I guess I wasn't sure after she took off for Vermont. And this is the first time she's been up to visit from Florida, isn't it?"

"She's still very fond of me," Dad says.

I don't say anything. I just drive him along as his happy chauffeur. How wonderful to have an unexpected upbeat moment. We've had so many up until this year. I have forgotten how much I enjoy him. In the backseat, Bea is clearing her throat. She leans forward.

"Did you tell your son what she asked you, Mr. Morris?"

"What did she ask you, Dad?"

He doesn't say anything. I pull up to a park on Long Island Sound and turn off the engine. He unbuckles his seat belt. I pull the key out of the ignition.

"She asked me to marry her," he says.

It takes a moment for it to sink in. I look at him. He looks at me. He isn't smiling, but there's something almost beatific about his face. His cheeks glow.

"What? She did not!"

"I was there," Bea says from the back. "She did. I heard her. Isn't that nice?"

My heart practically flies out of my mouth to do a little hora on the dashboard. Somebody still loves him as much as I do, I think. He's still a catch to her! I'm overjoyed.

"See that, Dad?"

"See what?"

"Doreen still loves you. She's been separated from you all fall and she has come to realize that life is better with you than without you."

"I guess that's true, isn't it?" he says.

"Even if you're not as spry as you were a year ago, she knows she'd rather have you around than not have you around! What a wonderful tribute to you. It's so great."

My father doesn't say anything. I can't figure out why.

Later I do, when I tell an uncle who's a lawyer about Doreen's proposal.

"Are his assets liquid?" he asks.

But even if she is after his money, I don't care. I still like Doreen and think she can save him by loving him, and if that means marriage, fine. But for Dad, marriage is out of the question. As a lawyer, he knows it makes no sense at his stage of life, and as a father who has my best interests at heart, he knows that he wants to leave me his savings because of my precarious finances.

"All I want is to continue keeping company with her," he says.

It isn't until the Bat Mitzvah when we really start to wonder what's going on with Doreen. She wants to attend, and she makes arrangements to fly up from Florida for the November weekend. But instead of staying with Dad in the luxury suite my brother has booked for them in a swank Manhattan hotel, she stays with a friend. And when my brother asks if she's willing to escort Dad around, she says she isn't planning on being in charge of him for the weekend.

"She did not say that," I tell Jeff.

"She did too," he says. "She wants to have fun without being weighed down. She suggested he bring Bea along to tend to his needs."

"He's not bringing Bea to the Bat Mitzvah," I yelp.

But he does. Bea is staying with him on the sofa of his grand hotel suite, where I have come to rehearse a song we will sing together for my niece, Maddy, at her luncheon reception the following day. It's to the tune of "My Heart Belongs to Daddy." He seems distracted as we go over his part. And he has not memorized the lyrics the way he promised he would.

"What's the matter, Dad? You don't want to sing?"

"I don't know if I'm feeling up to it."

"But we promised we'd do it—you can't let everyone down. This is our tradition."

He sighs. "I know, I know, but I don't know if I can manage."

"It's a nice occasion. You're here. Doreen is here. Why aren't you happy?"

He looks away from me. He shakes his head.

"Mr. Morris is feeling tired, that's all," Bea says.

"Is that all?" I ask.

"And he wishes Doreen would spend more time with him this weekend."

"Where is she, anyway?"

"Out with friends at a museum," Dad says.

Seeing his dejected face, I start to wonder about Doreen, not resent her, exactly, which my brother and his wife are quicker to do, but just question her motivations. What are the proper expectations to have with someone like her? Is she more a courtesan or friend than someone to consider family? They only had one good year. Why should she stick around for his decline? On the other hand, how can she be playing this half-in, half-out game? But then again, isn't half a Doreen better than none? His thoughts of her when she isn't around keep the seasonal cold out. It's his first winter up north in a dozen years or more, and he is dreading it.

We are standing in front of several hundred guests at the Bat Mitzvah luncheon to sing our parody. It's an impressive catering room on top of a fancy hotel. The Manhattan skyline, with Broadway and Carnegie Hall, is behind us. I hold a paper for him because he can't remember the lyrics we wrote together. My arm is around him. I tap his shoulder and we sing.

Some kids can be quite slovenly
Or they can be terribly bratty

But she's a pearl, Bat Mitzvah girl,
And our heart belongs to Maddy!

I look up and see some smiles, but not many. My brother and his wife seem to be forcing appreciation. My niece is looking down. Dad and I have never failed at our parody routine, yet today we are tanking. He stops halfway through the song. I squeeze him tight, my comrade, and we sputter through to the end. "Nicely done," I tell him as I escort him back to his table.

"I think I'm ready to go back to my hotel room," he says.

In January, much to our consternation, he announces plans to spend his March birthday week in Palm Beach. Doreen isn't hosting him, so he will stay in a hotel. He's too weak to get around on his own, and his aide isn't willing to go with him. So when he calls to remind us a month before the trip to book hotel and flights, it throws my brother and me. Flights are so expensive in high season, hotels too. Reservations should have been made a year ago.

"You know, Dad, it's not a good time, everything is booked," I say.

A mistake. He's intent on going, unstoppable as a spawning salmon.

"You made a promise and I expect you to keep it," he says one day in February, when I have taken him down to his lobby. "I'm counting on you to come through for me."

"But it's just not a good time, Dad."

"It's never a good time for you, Bobby."

"What is that supposed to mean?"

"Just what I said. You're overcommitted with all your projects when you should be spending more time with me. You're giving me short shrift and I think you know it."

I feel pierced by this remark from out of the blue.

"But I visit more than any kid in this building," I say.

"Maybe so, but I would like to see more of you."

Aaaagh! Am I actually hearing this after all the precious time I give him?

"You did this to yourself. You put yourself in a wheelchair and refuse to get out."

"That has nothing to do with my wanting to see more of you."

"It has everything to do with it. You're bored. You're lonely. You can't get around without help because you gave up on walking. And you've made yourself into a black box of misery and I'm your only form of entertainment. It's a lot for you to ask of me."

I know I should press down on my rage, but it's impossible now.

"Your time should be saved for me," he says.

"But I have a life. My work is important."

Perhaps too important. The solo show about his dating travails and how they intersected with mine is getting a reading by a prominent theater company, something I've wanted my whole life. But it isn't going well.

"You have to prioritize, Bobby," Dad says while waving an arthritic finger.

"This show could be a big deal for me—a lot is riding on it."

"Maybe so, but I'm going to tell you something you may not want to hear."

"What's that?"

"You're no Tom Cruise."

"What?"

"Or Neil Simon. Or even Harvey Fierstein."

"Did I say I was?"

I go hot with something between shame and rage.

"You have to face facts. It's not that I'm not proud of you, you know I am and you know I carry clippings of your newspaper columns to show people wherever I go."

Indeed he does—even when it embarrasses me to the point of mortification.

"But, Bobby, I have to tell you that as your biggest fan, I don't necessarily see that things will work out for you the way you keep hoping they will. Someone has to tell you that. You're not young. You're into your middle age. Journalism may be as far as you go."

"All my life I wanted a one-man show."

"But will anything come of it? I've watched you struggle for years. I hate seeing you write things that you don't get paid for only to be disappointed when they don't work out. I know you want to get into show business—I've watched you try to do it your whole life. Maybe someday you'll surprise me and it will happen, who's to say it won't? But I wish you would concentrate a lot less on all your side projects right now and save the extra time for me."

Like a cannon firing at the enemy, my hand launches a magazine on the coffee table in front of us, and it hits a wall, then splatters like a duck that's been shot in midair. It falls with a thud to the floor. "I come out to see you every week—I thought you liked my visits," I bark.

"I do when you aren't rushing out the door the moment you get here."

"Is that what you think I'm doing?"

I am ready to throttle him even though a part of me knows how right he is—that my visits are often full of e-mailing and worrying about work rather than him. The hour and a half it takes to get to him and the hour and a half it takes to get home don't matter to him. He wants more time. He wants someone not just to go out to dinner with or sing at the piano with but to sit around with playing Scrabble and watching TV. He's lonely. I know it, and because I can't accept responsibility for it, I keep pushing him to try the building's physical therapy, book discussions, bingo, and dance classes. I won't help him die, but I'm not really willing to help him live either. He wants more of me. And he wants Florida for his birthday with me too.

"You made me a promise. You said you'd go down there with me in March and I expect you to honor it," he's yelling. "I don't need lip service right now. I need commitment."

I don't know what to say. So I shoot up from his couch.

Then I grab my coat and walk out the lobby door into the freezing cold night to the Great Neck station to go home.

"He's got a lot of nerve," my brother says when I call from the train.

"I'm trying so hard to be a presence, but he's like a black hole of need."

"You're doing great. And there's something sweet about this, hard as it is for you."

"What's that? What could be sweet about feeling so guilty?"

"Don't you see it?"

"See what? What is it?"

"He adores you."

The train goes into a tunnel, and the whoosh of it hits me as hard as the observation.

Last Lap

I like LaGuardia Airport. It's small. It's also manageable in a way that life is not. In mid-March of 2006, I'm boarding a plane to join my father in Palm Beach. Lifting off over the skyline, I feel a little resentful about having to drop everything in the city below to be at his side for his eighty-third-birthday week down there. But he has demanded it, and my brother and I are splitting the time.

Maybe I'm using the excuse of work as a way to avoid admitting that my father has become the only important work I have to do right now. So many kids don't have it this easy with aging parents. They have children to care for, overwhelming expenses, and demanding jobs. I have none of that. My father even has an aide, but just not for this trip. For this trip he needs his sons. The plane banks south. *Florida!* I push back into my seat and sigh, thinking: *so depressing!* But for my dad it is a triumphant return to the land of his glory days—the American Dream with heaping servings of old friends and early-bird specials. This is to be Dad's last lap. He wants to dance with the wolves, run with the bulls, flap with the flamingos—be back where he belongs one last glorious time. And heaven help him, he needs me to help him do it.

On the eleventh floor of the Ritz-Carlton on the strip of high-rises south of Palm Beach, I knock on his door. No answer, but it's unlocked, so I walk in and step over T-shirts, socks, soiled tissues, magazines, and towels hanging off chairs like Spanish moss. In the corner he's parked his wheelchair, which he uses as a utility cart. It has a roll of paper towels hanging off one handle. In the bathroom, I see a dozen pill bottles and a portable commode—a toilet with legs and a purpose I don't quite understand. It's new in his trousseau.

He's asleep on an expansive bed in khaki shorts, tennis shirt, and cardigan. His legs no longer have hair, and it strikes me that mine, in my mid-forties, are going the same way. Above the air conditioning on full arctic blast, his snore soars to operatic heights.

"Dad?" He shifts on his bed but doesn't answer. He looks fragile, which scares me, but also, if I tilt my head another way, rested and handsome, with hair as white as dental floss hanging over his unlined face and prominent nose. I'm happy for him. He made it here, an improbable journey he's talked about for months. But I'm still aggravated that he insisted on dragging me into it. My brother has left a note by the phone.

Bob, Sorry I missed you. Had to get back to NY.
I arranged a late checkout tomorrow at 1 p.m. Bill is
paid. Have fun and good luck! Jeff

"Fun?" I mutter.
I am here to be his aide-de-camp.
A son with benefits.

"Your fingers are so cold," Doreen is saying. "Let me warm
them."

It's Thursday, my first night and his third, and we're at
dinner at the Ritz now, seated in a taupe banquette. Their
hands—hers well manicured, his otherwise—rest entwined
on the table.

I'm happy for him. He craves her affection.

"That feels wonderful," he sighs as she squeezes his hand.
"Couldn't be better."

"I'm so glad you're here, Joe," she says.

I drink my cocktail. They coo, cuddle, and split a dinner.
I have always liked her. She's cultured, yet unpretentious and
youthful in outlook. What I like about her most, though, is
how much she likes my father. Or seems to at this moment,
anyway. When she fell for him, she turned his life from a
lonely existence into a high-octane lark.

The Ritz, where we're eating tonight, is expensive, with
one of those narrative menus that takes too long to read. But

my father, who just a year ago would get in his car to hunt down any bargain meal, is too weak to leave the hotel. He's happy, eyes gleaming, smile wide.

"Heaven," he coos in her ear. "I'm in heaven."

I'm not. Because it's a busy time of year in South Florida, and we booked everything so late, we'll be moving from one place to another for the next three days. Doreen has not invited Dad to stay at her big apartment up the road.

"I just don't understand why she can't put him up," Jeff had said.

"I guess she wants the romance but not the responsibility," I told him.

I can't blame her. The man she was running around with just last year has become so old.

"Don't you think she's yanking his chains?"

"Yeah, but he's happy knowing she still has feelings for him, period."

"Is that what you call it when she can't even put him up in her guest room?"

Jeff can be fiercely protective. Anyone who interferes with the family happiness has to be scrutinized and skewered.

"Whatever it is, it gives him a lift, a little hope, better than nothing," I told him.

"Yeah, I guess you're right," he conceded.

The lovebirds split a piece of cheesecake on a raspberry coulis splatter. He slurps his decaf, she sips hers. The dinner bill goes to my brother's credit card, a gift from afar. Then, bringing the night to an abrupt end almost without warning, Doreen kisses us good-bye and goes off to her car to drive away. It's hard not to feel as if she's ditching him. But when I study his face across the table as she leaves the dining room, I can't find much disappointment.

Her presence has elevated him more than any antidepressant. I have to be grateful.

I wheel him through the hotel lobby. Other families are saying good night, children and grandchildren. Well-put-together grandparents—his age but still fit—make me feel resentful of their good health. But then, I've always been jealous of other people's families. Did my father really have to end up in a wheelchair? I am convinced he gave up walking too soon. I push him to the elevator, where we wait with a senior couple who don't look their age.

"Marvelous weather," my father says. "Just glorious."

"Yes, it is," the man replies. "Isn't it?"

In his room, Dad presses me into service right away, using me as something between a baby nurse and a butler. I help him out of his wheelchair and find his pajamas buried under a pile in the closet. "Do you need help getting them on?" I ask.

"No, I can do it," he says. "It takes a while, but I can."

That's good. What grown son wants to get so close to the body of a father in such decline? Or, in fact, to his father at any time? But while the idea of helping him pull up his pajama bottoms makes me uncomfortable, so does watching him do it himself. He bends so slowly to get them, and then he can barely reach. He puffs, snorts, and sighs.

"There, see that? I did it," he says.

"Good job, Dad!"

"Thank you, Bobby!"

He struggles onto the edge of his bed and he grunts, first lowering his body carefully, then slowly lying down against his pillow with his feet still on the floor. It is such an effort, each movement a test of strength. I feel a surge of tenderness that makes me want to run over to him and tousle his hair and tell him "Good job" again as if he were a little boy.

"Let me help you get your feet up," I say.

Soon enough he'll have a portable oxygen tank at his side all day long. For now, he fights for breath as I take one leg and lift it. Then I do the other, just as I did for my mother so often in her last years. His loud sigh reminds me of hers.

"That's wonderful, thank you very much."

I pull a sheet up over him, then a cotton blanket. He takes my hand.

"You're doing marvelously on your first night," he says. "A real help."

"My pleasure," I say, pressing down on my sadness.

"I worry I'm too much for you," he says.

"Not at all, Dad."

After turning off his bedside light, I sit down at a cluttered desk and clear a small space to mark up some work from my briefcase. But he interrupts.

"You know, I could use some Kleenex."

"No problem," I say as I go over and place them nearer to him.

"And also my pills, if you don't mind."

"Yes, sir." I find them and hand them to him.

"You're welcome," I say before he can thank me.

How is it possible that getting these things for him is anything but an honor?

I'm not a sound sleeper, and like him, I snore. So instead of getting into the bed next to his, I pull some pillows and blankets out to the balcony. I like fresh air as much as he dislikes it. And sleeping in such close proximity makes me squeamish. It always has. I'm not good at intimacy, and I often find myself doing whatever I can to keep anyone who needs me at bay. Happily, Ira, who is as demonstrative as he is generous as a spouse, has changed some of that. I miss him tonight. The moon, full and the color of a matzoh ball, moves through a thin soup of cirrus clouds. The waves come in, go out, their sound like a lullaby about good real estate.

It's been a long day, and I fall asleep.

Several hours later, long before sunrise, Dad wakes me with a loud clearing of his throat while sitting on the edge of his bed. I look inside the room and see his head and hair hanging down while he stares at his bare feet. Perhaps he's trying to move his legs but can't. He doesn't go anywhere. Has he been wondering where I am? Wanting me to help him to the bathroom?

"Dad, what is it?" I whisper as I step in from the balcony.

"There you are, Bobby. I need a hand to get to the john."

I rush to his side to lift him up, facing him as if he were a dance partner. It's as intimate as we've ever been, almost cheek to cheek. He's up on his feet now, steadying himself, and I help him walk, then help him sit down on the toilet. He manages to lower his pajama bottoms himself.

"I'll just be a little while," he says as I turn away.

"Okay, I'll wait for you. I'm right here."

I am starting to understand what it must be like for his home care aide to have to do this all week, never really able to sleep through the night or claim her own time. And I can't imagine what it must be like for all the caring sons and daughters doing this full-time in their homes.

I help him back to bed, and not long after that we are both asleep again.

I dream I am a boy in his arms in a swimming pool surrounded by palm trees. His hair is thick and dark. His chest wide, his stance firm. He lifts me up onto his shoulders and I hold on to his head. Then he sends me shrieking in an arc through the air and into the water.

Morning comes to the Ritz, with the sun rising from the ocean over the building's imposing faux-Spanish façade and throwing golden light over our room. I'm pleased to see Dad has dressed himself in khaki shorts and a clean white tennis shirt with a pocket for his pens. Only his feet are bare. Getting socks and shoes on is a daily challenge.

"Good morning," he calls.

"How are you feeling?"

"Never better!"

Breakfast in the hotel's upstairs VIP lounge is complimentary—for him, a lover of free things, nirvana. He stuffs himself, and when he's done, I wheel him back to the room to pack. We're moving to another hotel in a couple of hours, a few buildings up the road. I don't have much to put back in my duffel. His situation is the opposite. Looking around the room, I take a deep breath. Then I zip around, stuffing everything into bags.

"Is this shirt dirty or clean, Dad?"

"Put that in clean."

"Looks dirty to me."

"I can wear it another time."

"Not around me, you can't."

A half hour later, everything is packed. We call the porter for help. "Don't forget the commode," Dad says. The commode, which I guess he brings along more for security than necessity, since he's been using the real toilet, is in the bathroom. There's no bag in the room big enough to hold it. So when the porter arrives, he places it with everything else on the luggage cart, whose fake brass wheels squeak as we ease down the dimly lit corridor and onto the elevator. A thin blonde with face work and an expensive pocketbook starts to step in on a lower floor. But when she sees the commode, she backs away.

"I'll wait for the next one," she says.

"Plenty of room," Dad says as the elevator doors close.

The porter stares straight ahead. I look down at my shoes. Dad whistles. It's mortifying—a toilet on a luggage cart. It's also hilarious, given the hauteur of the hotel. People pay so much attention to their outfits here and everything reeks of luxury, but Dad is oblivious to the status indicators. In the lobby people look at our unseemly cart of stuff, then look away. And at the grand entrance, we get into the white Lincoln he rented. It's a yacht of a car, and I'm not sure where to go with him now. We can't check into the next hotel for hours.

"What about lunch?" he asks.

"We just had breakfast."

"It'll pass the time."

We find a café near a public beach and order grilled chicken sandwiches. He looks so happy in his white wicker chair, just sitting with me doing nothing. My heel taps under the table.

"So what's on the agenda at your birthday dinner tomorrow?" I ask.

His mouth is full. But that doesn't stop him from answering.

"Nothing special from what I can tell, just some of Doreen's friends coming to dinner."

"Nobody you know is coming, none of your old pals?"

"Your aunt Sylvia is coming," he says.

That's his eighty-eight-year-old sister from up the road. "And nobody else you know?"

"I'm not sure. It's up to Doreen."

This strikes me as odd. It's his birthday, after all, and he's here to see his old friends, so why wouldn't she give him a say about the guest list? On the other hand, it's generous of her to make him a dinner. I look at my watch—two hours until the next hotel check-in.

"Hey, do you want to write something to sing together?"

His fork, trembling slightly in his hand, hits his plate.

"That would be wonderful. I'd love it."

We've had more success at playing the lowbrow parodists than anything else, including doubles games of tennis, in which my murderous rages turned me into a suburban Hamlet. Trying to let him teach me bridge was another well-intentioned disaster.

We pick a song to parody, an old-time melody in a minor key about Yussel (a man with Dad's name, Joseph, in Yiddish). I jot down lyrics as we invent them together. It's trial and error but without any of the conflict or bickering that plague us when deciding where to eat dinner or which route to take to the airport. I write and rewrite. When he puts in his two cents, I surprise myself by listening. Then, with a second draft I've written on Ritz-Carlton stationery in the neat handwriting of someone in the opposite of a hurry, we sing the words aloud sotto voce.

Oy, Yussel, Yussel, how's it feel to grow up?
At eighty-three you're more than halfway there

Oy, Yussel, Yussel, Yussel, time is fleeting
Fortunately you still have lots of hair

A few people at a nearby table look us up and down. I sing more loudly, and that encourages him to do the same.

So listen, Yussel, everyone still loves you
Although you snore more than a little bit
You don't dance the way you did
But at bridge you still can bid
Yussel, Yussel, you're just an old kid!

It's silly, but we are two frustrated hams who have always shared the need for attention, and our voices go as well together as horseradish and gefilte fish. Despite the inconvenience of the trip, I am happy to be here now, wasting time together in this significant, insignificant way.

He is beaming and years fall off him.

"You're knocking it out of the park today," he says.

By the time we check into hotel number two, it's late in the afternoon. Doreen has other plans for the night, and he's too exhausted to go out with his sister. The bedtime routine is just like the night before, with the added activity of bathing. I have never helped him into a shower—Bea, his aide back home, has always done that—and I have not gotten so close to his naked body since he tossed me around the pool when I was a child. He needs help stepping into the shower stall now.

"Ready," he calls to me.

I open the bathroom door and find him with a bath towel wrapped around his fragile body. I don't want to look, but I can't help noticing he has the same small moles that I've been getting on my back in recent years. He is, I know, my genetic destiny and a window into my future. For years he aged beautifully, with a young face and disposition that gave me hope for my own old age. Now he sags in flesh and spirit. I step in and give him my hand. He takes it.

"Here we go, Dad," I whisper.

There really is nothing to it, just giving him my hand for a few steps that make all the difference and help him feel secure. I test the shower water to make sure it's warm enough.

"Okay, time to get in," I say. "Let me take your towel."

I pull it off and, while avoiding looking directly at him, take his hand and hold it as he steps into the spray of warm water. There is no safety bar. I reach for a cake of soap to give him, unwrap it, and then step away, but stay on high alert, ready to pounce if he slips. He doesn't. And moments later, as steam surrounds me and he emerges like a Jewish phantom from a steam room, I help him get out. He smells of lavender. I hand him a towel and start to dry him.

"That's okay, I can do it," he says.

When he's dry, I give him his clean underwear and pajamas.

"Maybe just a hand getting into the bottoms," he says.

We walk to his bed. He lowers himself to sit. I lower my

head and, holding my breath, put the pajamas (sky-blue cotton shorties) on at his feet and pull them up. They slip on easily.

"Thanks, I have it now," he says. "That's wonderful, just wonderful."

And so it goes. I get him his pills. I fill his water glass and find him the empty Snapple bottle he likes to have by his bedside in case he can't make it to the bathroom in the middle of the night. ("It's the Lasix, it makes me have to go," he explains.) Finally, when I've turned out his light and settle into reading a magazine, and hear only the sea and the humming of the ventilation system, he calls out for one last thing, another blanket. I bring one to him, spreading it out over him the way my mother used to do for me years ago. I feel as if I should be saying a blessing as it floats down over him. Or maybe singing him a lullaby while cradling his head in my arms.

"You're doing so well," he says.

"Nothing to it," I reply.

Something in me has shifted. I don't feel annoyed as his requests keep coming. I feel something else, something that surprises me as it creeps up. Is it tenderness? Someone I know once suggested that most infirm people become very sweet by necessity—so that the healthy people around them will love them more and want to take care of them. My father has been unusually sweet and appreciative since I arrived here in Florida, and he is making me feel so useful.

Even if it's manipulative, it's nice. Just for a day or so, there is nothing else to worry about except him. It's Friday night, and the workweek is over—no need to worry about any-thing or anyone in the world but him. Ira is in New York in the apartment we just bought—another declaration of our intention of building a life together. He e-mails encouraging messages. He tells me what he's buying for our new place to make it pop. He cares about design.

I'm glad it's just Dad and me here, away from all that now.

The balcony at this hotel, a considerable downgrade from the Ritz, is too small for sleeping. So tonight I have no choice but the twin bed right beside my father's in this tiny room. He's snoring with mouth open wide enough to swallow the sky. I don't want to disturb him, tell him to stop it or even roll him over. Instead I turn the fan on for white noise, put my earplugs in, and read a magazine. Even though I think it's going to be impossible to fall asleep, I drift off soon enough, and have a dream of my mother, giving me a bath as a child. She is the young beauty captured again and again in our home movies, the one who disappeared behind her illness, which aged and ravaged her before her time had come to be old.

I wake up to the light of morning. Dad is already dressed.

"Happy birthday, Dad," I say. "How are you feeling?"

"Never better," he says.

I'm surprised to find myself feeling the same way.

*   *   *

After breakfast downstairs, it's time, heaven help me, to pack him up again and get out. It's quicker this time than the day before, when we left the Ritz. The only issue in checking out is the bill. "I didn't make this phone call," he says as he looks at a printout.

The charge is for three dollars. The desk clerk looks miffed. I tell Dad to let it go.

"Keep out of this," he says.

I reach for my wallet to reimburse him and beg him not to make things harder.

"It's the principle," he says.

It takes twenty minutes for someone in the office to straighten it out, and it throws me back into a testy mood as we exit the lobby. I tip the valet and get behind the wheel of the white rental Lincoln, and can't help feeling we're being exiled—banished from another nice hotel in high season. Tonight, after his birthday dinner at Doreen's apartment, we will be moving into the home of my aunt Bev in North Palm Beach, about half an hour away. It seems an eternity from now. The car sails along, smooth as a cruise ship on South Ocean Boulevard. Seniors in tracksuits are power-walking on either side of us as pelicans drift overhead. I push the button to put all the windows down. Dad pushes the button to put them all up. "What do you have against fresh air, anyway?" I ask.

"Pollen, for one thing, so let's use the air conditioner."

He turns the fan up too high. Outside his window a turquoise swath of ocean goes on for an eternity—like the day ahead. Outside my window, white high-rise buildings throw shade across the road. Exuberant flowers are blooming along the sidewalks. The isolation from the world is complete inside this hermetically sealed gas-guzzler. His birthday dinner is still several hours away. What to do until then? We drive up the A1A to Boynton Beach, past the synagogue where he used to sing in the choir with Mom. He points out the weedy municipal park in a poor section of Lantana where he pulled up with me years ago to toss tennis balls and old rackets to kids from his trunk—classic Joe Morris generosity. He was always so happy here, his spiritual homeland.

We eat lunch. We eat ice-cream cones. We buy wine for Doreen's dinner. We find an oldies station on the radio that we both like. I'm his driver, his jester. And all I want for his birthday is to keep the despair that has been plaguing him since last summer far away.

"Hey, what do you want for your birthday, Dad?"

"Your presence is enough of a present," he jokes.

"I have an idea. What about shoes without backs?"

"What do you mean? Slippers?"

"They're called slides. You don't have to bend over to put them on, you can just step into them. For indoors or out. You can even wear them without socks."

"That sounds great," he says. "Where can we find them?"

Over another bridge and the Intracoastal Waterway, we end up in the little city of Lake Worth, the poor cousin to

Palm Beach. I leave him in the car in a parking lot that looks seedy, with some vagrants hanging out by a Dumpster. But what the hell, he'll be fine.

"You sure you don't want to come in, Dad?"

"No, I'll wait here and listen to the radio."

"I don't want to have to return them if they don't fit."

"They'll fit, go ahead, take your time."

Inside the one shoe store in town, I find a pair. They're black and basic but not cheap at $150. I had hoped to spend about half of that. My hands get clammy holding them while I try to decide what to do. I can afford $150. But I stand there paralyzed, unable to buy them. I've spent twice as much on shoes for myself. But for something so useful for my old man?

"Thanks anyway," I tell the clerk, and bolt for the door.

On the sidewalk, I see some crystal lamps in a consignment shop window two doors down. I have just moved into a new apartment with Ira, who has ramped up my design consciousness in a way I never thought possible. My father adores him and tells me over and over how glad he is that I've finally met my soul mate. Our plan is to take our new white apartment in a Palm Beach grandma direction, with chandeliers and beveled mirrors. So like a decorator moth, I'm drawn inside the shop, and suddenly, my soulful trip for some useful shoes becomes a fevered, gleeful search for vintage lamps. After pillaging the aisles, I find three, which take a long time to bubble-wrap at checkout. By the time

I walk out of the store, three-quarters of an hour have passed, and I'm ecstatic carrying my carefully wrapped box of bling.

When I get to the car I expect to find Dad asleep, mouth ajar and snoring. But he isn't. He's wide-eyed and agitated. A few beads of sweat dot his forehead.

"Where were you?" he rasps.

"What do you mean? You know—shopping for shoes."

"What took you so long?"

"What's the matter, Dad?"

I feel some annoyance at his annoyance.

"I'm thirsty. It's hot in this car. I've been waiting an hour."

"I'm sorry."

"Why so long? You said you'd be a few minutes."

How can I tell him that I opted to shop for myself after not getting anything for him?

"What's in your box?" he asks as I pull out of the parking lot.

"What box? Oh, that. That's just some stuff. For the apartment."

"I'm very thirsty," he says. "And I need to get to a bathroom."

I want to suggest that even as his handservant I have rights too, and that if I want to leave him for an hour with the radio on, the doors locked, and the windows open for air, it's not the end of the world. As we drive, I can see my mother in the backseat with the traumatized look on her face she'd get when Dad and I would fight over nothing. The sun streams into the car in the back from the west. It casts a harsh light.

When we pull up to the parking lot of Doreen's apartment building, Dad is all smiles, anticipating the evening ahead. She's standing in her parking area, looking youthful at seventy-five in the flattering golden late-afternoon glow of Florida springtime.

"You boys are right on time," she says as I pull his wheelchair out of the trunk.

"Special occasion," he says. "Can't be late."

He looks up at her from his car seat.

"Happy birthday, Joey," she says as she leans down to kiss his cheek.

With my hands under him, I hoist him up and help him into his wheelchair.

"Okay?" I ask.

"Never better!"

He reaches out to Doreen and she takes his hand.

"This is the night I've been waiting for," he says.

"I'm just getting the salad ready," she says. "We can visit while I chop."

"Anything you say, dear."

I can't help noticing how his whole demeanor changes— he gets younger and so courtly around her. She looks at him and then a cloud crosses her face as she leans in, frowns, and lets go of his hand. "Oh, no," she says.

"What?" he asks.

"You didn't shave?"

"I shaved last night."

"You can't come to my dinner unshaven, Joe. Do you have a razor with you?"

"I think he looks okay," I say. "His suitcase is going to be hard to pull out."

It's buried in the trunk behind my obscenely heavy box of bling, and wedged in the far recesses beyond his walker and his commode. Having already loaded and unloaded his stuff twice over the past two days as we played our no-room-at-the-inn game (Joseph and Bobby), I really don't want to dig anything out until we get to my aunt Bev's at the end of the night.

"He really does look fine to me," I say.

"If he has a razor blade," she says, "please get it."

"Of course we can, right away, no problem," I say.

"That's my boy," Dad says.

A half hour later, I'm at a nearby Kmart shopping for a giant duffel bag so that I can get my box of bling home on my flight tomorrow. There's still some time before the dinner party. I'm also looking to spend about forty dollars on a birthday present for the man who took me on family vacations, sent me to summer camp, put me through college, and still offers to lend me money. While I'm in the checkout line, my phone rings. "Bobby, where the heck are you?"

He sounds winded and upset.

"Shopping. What's the matter, Dad?"

"I need you here right now."

"I'm fifteen minutes away."

"Why did you go so far?"

The problem is that he's in Doreen's bathroom on the toilet and unable to stand up without a hand. He's too ashamed to call for her help. I run to the car and gun it back to her building, where I find her in the bathroom, helping him, exactly the humiliating scenario he wanted to avoid. He winces as she helps him pull up his khaki trousers. She looks over at me.

"I'll let you take it from here," she says as she leaves us.

I step up to help him. His hand is shaking. His face is flushed with rage, while mine is pinched into a false look of passivity, pretending that little is wrong.

"I can do it," he snaps.

"Okay, just trying to help."

"Just trying to help means not going away when I ask you to stay close."

"Oh, come on, Dad."

"Come on nothing, I was counting on you to be here."

He's right. And I can't imagine the indignity of a shrunken life viewed mostly at waist level from a wheelchair—the effort it takes him just to get into a car or onto a plane, the absolute certainty that nothing will be easy again, including, in his case, trying to die. But even with all that in my mind, I'm still angry that he's demonizing me. I step back to give him some room, stand against the bathroom door. The doorbell gongs in Doreen's foyer and her greetings ring out as guests arrive. It's a large bathroom, twice as large as any we've shared in our hotels, and while it occurs to me again that this is where he should be staying this week, it also hits me that this icky incident that Doreen has just witnessed and addressed—helping a man she loves off a toilet seat, a man who not all that long ago was her great new able-bodied romance—this is exactly what she wanted to avoid having to do in her home. I should have been here with him. I blew it.

Dad finishes tucking in his shirt and buckling his belt. But he doesn't turn from the mirror. Rather, he leans into it, his hands resting on the counter, his freshly shaven face frozen in a grimace. Is he unable to move or is he just staring life down?

"You okay?"

"Just taking a moment."

I run, fix him a drink—a vodka and orange juice—and present it to him. He rarely drinks.

"I'm not supposed to," he says.

"Make an exception tonight, birthday boy."

I watch him take a sip and nod. He sips again, then smiles. I feel tension leave my body and feel relief to be of use again. He's going to be okay now, and he's willing to enjoy the night.

"Delicious," he says. "Hits the spot." Then he drinks it all down.

*   *   *

Unfortunately, the party isn't all that much of one. Yes, his sister is there, as is a couple from Long Island who have some memories to share. But most of the guests are Doreen's friends, not his. Just like an adolescent with bad manners, I have a hard time feigning interest or answering their questions. I keep trying to get them to turn their questions to Dad. But there's no fuss over him, the birthday boy, at all. And perhaps that's nothing to find offensive—he's eighty-three tonight, not three. Just a few years ago, six months after my mother had died, we made a huge fuss for him right down the road at an eightieth birthday party. It was a major event, even as it felt as if we were erasing the memory of our mother way too soon. But it was what he wanted.

After I help Doreen clear the plates and an overcooked roast, it's time for Dad and me to sing the parody we wrote. Because I don't know most of the guests, I feel anxious. It doesn't help that Doreen's electric piano is out of whack. But Dad rises to the occasion, singing like a star, and when we finish I have tears of pleasure in my eyes. Nobody even applauds, not even my aunt Sylvia. And Doreen is busy getting a birthday cake ready. She walks out of the kitchen and places it in front of Dad as we sing to him. A dozen candles illuminate his face. He looks like a happy boy of eight, not eight decades. He doesn't have the strength to blow out all the candles at once. He puffs at them one at a time.

After the last guest leaves, I wheel him into the kitchen,

where he watches as I help Doreen clean up. She's still perky. Her apron is unsoiled except for one spot of gravy.

"Wasn't that a wonderful party?" she asks.

"It couldn't have been better," Dad says. "I'm walking on air."

It's time to get going. Much as I'd still like to leave him here with her, I know now that it's impossible. She has been gracious to make him a dinner, and we should be grateful for the kindness. She hasn't been in his life all that long. And we've known for months that while there was a momentary question of the possibility, they aren't getting married.

I accept a slab of leftover cake, run to the car, and throw his Dopp kit back into the trunk with the intensity of someone moving out after a fight. Then, a little breathless, I come back to wheel Dad away. At Doreen's door, he reaches for her hand, draws her down to him, and kisses her cheek. She kisses him back, and I feel thankful she has done as much as she can and in her own way. The idea of love is still there, frail as the petal of a lily surviving late into the season.

As I drive us up I-95, past the airport and chain hotels that he likes but that I would not allow on this trip, I am starting to feel some relief. I will be going home tomorrow. But what is this other feeling? Regret to be going so soon? I look over and see him working his teeth with a toothpick, a habit acquired in recent years (proving that old dogs can learn new tricks). He seems so happy. Despite its rocky start, the night was a success, just as our others here have been.

He's having fun down here, insisting on it, and I have to admire him for that.

Aunt Bev and Uncle Howie live in a golfing community north of Palm Beach, one of those places far from town and full of cul-de-sacs, sprinkler systems, and the occasional alligator in a man-made lake. It's late when we pull up to their stucco ranch. I turn off the engine and put my head on the steering wheel, psyching myself into unpacking the car one last time. Aunt Bev, stalwart, seventy, and in jeans and a sweater, holds her screen door open. Howie is away.

"I'm so sick of this," I hiss.

"But you're just here with him three days," she whispers.

"I know, I know. But being his helper is harder than you think."

Her smile disappears. "You don't know hard," she says.

Aunt Bev watched her mother die of breast cancer when she was a teenager. And now she is watching her daughter, Julie, dying of the same disease. Actually, watching isn't the word. She isn't watching. She's been crisis-managing all winter, flying back and forth to Long Island, pushing herself to the limit, shuttling the grandchildren to lessons, babysitting and getting Julie to her various appointments—chemo, scans, consultations—handling endless responsibilities and aggravations because of a prolonged and increasingly hopeless fight against the inevitable. Julie, a sweet forty-three-year-old, is at stage four. Aunt Bev has taken on her duties

without complaint. She handles everything with quiet effi-
ciency, the opposite of my approach. She's rarely in Florida
these days, much as she loves it and her golf down here in
winter.

I move Dad into the big, well-appointed room he'll
occupy for a week, where he falls asleep. At the other end
of the house, Aunt Bev and I sit in her recently remodeled
kitchen. She offers me a rugelach and makes me a cup of
tea. The fridge hums, and outside, a few crickets chirp in
the subtropical darkness. We talk about life, about my life,
mostly, and it reminds me how much I miss my mother and
our times alone in her kitchen late at night when she leaned
in on every word. The history I have with Aunt Bev, her sister, goes deep. Her daughters and my brother and I grew
up together, and memories of holidays, overnights, and special occasions run on a continual nostalgic loop. We are in
each other's movies and albums, a family with few emotional
complications. But how will Aunt Bev endure my father and
his needs all week, knowing her own daughter is in such terrible shape up north?

"He's not an imposition to *endure*," she says. "Are you
kidding?"

"Why would I be kidding?"

"He's my brother-in-law. I've known him fifty years.
Don't you know how he took care of me before I was
married?"

I tell her I don't remember.

"I was young and single when my mother died," she said.

"And your father made me feel so welcome in the house with your mother. He gave me driving lessons and got me into his tennis games. Then when Howie was starting out, and he had no work, he found him clients and set him up with an office at his law firm. And he was so wonderful to your cousin George too."

Cousin George was the troubled son of my mother's other sister.

"He never thought twice about helping people out," she says. "He wanted to do it."

I look in on my father before going to sleep. His snoring is gentle tonight and he looks so at peace, at home in someone's home, welcome and loved. He's enjoying himself so much he's extending his trip and is going to stay on for a while, then fly home in a few weeks with a new aide, who will start the day after tomorrow.

I leave him the next day, knowing he's in good hands. And as my flight soars over Palm Beach, with its lush wetlands, pastel buildings, and turquoise waters, I think about what Aunt Bev said about his wanting to make so many people feel so welcome. Then I look out the window and wave down to him below.

"Happy birthday, old man," I whisper.

I have a feeling it will be his last.

Redemption

The call comes on the Sunday of Memorial Day weekend, a couple of months after Dad has returned from his triumphant Palm Beach visit and is back in Great Neck at his assisted living apartment. It's from Ralph, the health care aide who has been looking after him this spring.

"He's in the hospital and I think you should come," Ralph says.

"What happened?"

"Heart failure, I found him on the floor."

"Are you sure?"

Dad's heart has been failing more and more, as his cardiologist predicted a year ago, and he's been landing overnight in hospitals with scares all spring.

"So you think it's really serious?" I ask Ralph.

"I'm not sure, but I think this may be the end."

There's panic in his voice, poor man, trying to do the right thing by getting me to come. But there have been several calls like this of late, all false alarms, and I'm in our house upstate and not inclined to make a long drive on a holiday weekend if it can wait. Is this really it?

"So you're saying he won't make it?"

Silence at the other end of the phone.

"Ralph?"

"I just think you should get down here right away."

We have houseguests and we're planning a party in the backyard for Monday. All I want is to enjoy my house with Ira in our mountain village, where, after a cold and rainy spring, everything is finally in full bloom. But I don't argue. My brother is out of the country. I'm the only child around. And no doubt Ralph would like to get home for the holiday too, without worrying that nobody is keeping my father company and advocating for him at the hospital. Maybe this is just Ralph's way of getting time off with his own family on a long weekend. I don't really know. But I tell him to go home and that I will be down there in four or five hours.

"You won't be sorry," he says. "I think it's the right thing to do."

Well, yes. Hospitals are lonely. To be near the end must be scary, even though the end is exactly what my father has been hoping for all year.

An hour later, I'm driving through a moonless night. The New York State Thruway is busy, Interstate 84 only a little less so as I weave in and out of traffic and try to find some music to make the drive go faster. All the public radio stations have bad news about the war in Iraq, which President Bush is still defending despite its unpopularity. My father still defends it too, as he supports the entire militaristic administration. "Idiots," I mutter. I'm speeding because I'm worried he'll die before I get to him. It could be happening as I grip the steering wheel with one hand, still scanning the radio for any song that will ease the tension. Is my father sleeping right now or gasping for his last breaths, the death rattle in his throat already started? Is he conscious or so pumped up with drugs that he is already adrift?

What will I tell him? How much I love him, despite his politics and all our conflicts? And is he wondering, *Where are my sons tonight? My boys?*

The traffic eases when I pass the exit for Beacon, and now there's nothing but darkness, and I floor it to eighty miles an hour. And then something in front of my car takes a second for me to comprehend. It's a large buck with antlers. Without thinking, I swerve hard to the right, avoiding him. A car in my blind spot almost hits me and blasts its horn in angry rebuke. "Shit!" I yell. "Shit shit shit shit shit!" My hands shake. If that deer had come a moment later or if that car had been one foot closer, I'd have been dead before my dad. But here I am spared, pondering my own mortality along with my father's. How long do I have? I wonder. My heart is likely to become erratic like his. My brother's already is. Soon we'll both be short of breath. Like a deer running from the darkness into the traffic, health trouble can strike anyone at any moment.

I drive a little more slowly and head south on I-684, then speed up after White Plains. I can't miss saying good-bye to the man who brought me up, who always made things right for me in his own hapless way. It's only been in these last months that we've let go of some of our quibbles and started to settle in for something resembling a loving father-son relationship. I don't ask him to cheer up anymore or dress in cleaner clothes. I take all his advice, no matter how silly it is, and rarely rush him off the phone the way I used to. I don't nag him to exercise anymore either. It's pointless now anyway. He's at peace as an invalid in a wheelchair who's never going to walk again. We both know it and accept his total inertia.

And now, if he's truly at the very end of his life, I want to be able to say a long, sweet good-bye, hold his hand, sing him a song. I wish I hadn't hesitated so long on the phone about coming. I wish I had been able to say *Yes, I'm coming right away. Yes, of course I'll be there for you, Dad.*

Visiting hours are over when I walk into North Shore hospital and ride up in an elevator to a cheerful floor with brightly painted walls. I'm scared and my breathing is rapid and shallow. What will my father look like? What will he be like? Able to even open his eyes to acknowledge me? Will he be able to talk? Will I be able to thank him for everything,

and apologize for being so cynical? Or will this be a time
to just listen, let him talk about his life and the regrets he
has and the apologies he wants to make? Maybe we'll be
able to have a conversation about the spirit, *his* spirit, a quiet
talk that will bring some closure to his life and this last,
long and difficult year, which he wants so much to come to
an end.

I find his name next to a door, knock, and with pounding heart, open it. I panic when I don't see him in a bed.
I'm too *late*, I think. It's over. He's gone and I never said
good-bye. Then I see something opposite the bed. Legs.
His legs. And at the end of them his Velcro-strapped gray
vinyl sneakers. He's sitting on the far side of the pale yellow
room, straight up in his wheelchair. And he isn't in a hospital gown but in his civilian clothes—khaki trousers, tennis
shirt, and lime-green V-neck sweater, which complements
the decor. Clear oxygen tubes are stuck into his nose, with a
small portable tank on little wheels like a rolling suitcase at
his side.

He's listening on his cell phone, grimacing. Then he
erupts.

"No, the issue is not the service; it's the amount of peak
minutes," he bellows. "There's a mistake on the bill and I've
been overcharged by fourteen dollars and seven cents."

He looks up to see me, then lights up with a big smile
and waves me closer. He gestures that I should move a pile
of clothes, magazines, takeout food, and newspapers off a

chair by the window. A Mets game is muted on the TV that hangs from chains on the ceiling.

"Look, I'm not arguing for anything other than what's right," he's saying. "I have no record of those calls, and it's impossible that I would make any during peak hours."

By his bedside a *Times* crossword page has a ring stain on it—Snapple or maybe from a mug of instant decaf. In his pocket a pen has leaked a dot of black onto his shirt. It's all business as usual with him, and not going to be the vigil I was expecting. It's not even the bed of a terminally ill person. My father's tone is escalating on the phone and his nostrils are starting to flare—not necessarily a bad thing. Aggravation is good for his blood pressure. He thinks it makes his heart stronger. He often tells us that a good argument makes him feel better, so maybe that's why he's been mouthing off so much lately, defending the Bush administration to the many liberal Democrats who populate this part of Long Island. He looks for excuses to get angry all the time now. Well, it shows the old man still has some life in him, whether he wants to admit it or not.

"I have serious health issues and this is very aggravating!" he yells into his phone. "I'm asking that you do the right thing, that's all. I'm not too old to switch my service."

He flashes a conspiratorial smile and I shake my head in mock disapproval. He nods.

"That's great, wonderful, thanks very much," he says, and clicks off the call.

I hardly know what to think. Not only is he not dying,

he has just brought his cell phone service provider to its knees, something not all that far from beating back death itself.

"Bobby, delighted to see you, I'm just thrilled," he says.

Even though I can see he's fine or at least not dead, I ask, "What happened, Dad?"

"Nothing serious, AT&T screwed up my bill."

"Not that. I mean what are you doing in the hospital?"

"Nothing so terrible. I lost my breath and fell in the apartment after lunch, that's all."

"But Ralph told me to come, and that you might not make it."

"Ralph can be very dramatic. But it's awfully nice to see you."

His voice is a little breathy, even with the oxygen supply coursing through the tubes in his nose. "How's your weekend going? I was hoping to see you. Were you in the city?"

"I was upstate," I say. "I almost hit a deer driving down here."

"You didn't have to trouble yourself. I'm not dying."

"Are you sure? I mean, do you promise?"

"I feel pretty good given my circumstances. I'm sure they'll send me home tomorrow."

I shift in my chair, cross my legs, uncross them, and then get up to throw away the trash he has managed to accumulate on both windowsill and bedside table. He turns up his ball game.

"I'm sorry about all this."

"What? About your mess or that you aren't dying?"

"I don't like to inconvenience you, that's all."

"Not at all, Dad, not at all."

What to do now? Even at the end, when it might finally be time to relent and give the man what he's wanted his whole life—a son for watching sports on TV with—I refuse to sit and stare at the game with him. It's just not my idea of quality time. Odd as it sounds, it's a little disappointing not to be able to have the end-of-life conversation I so frantically scripted on my drive—the one that so many spiritually obsessed boomers think is essential at a death even if the dying find it unnecessary and intimidating. I want to squeeze some meaning out of this visit, something that will lift it above the rest, something if not exactly sacred then at least transitional, or, better yet, redemptive, like that character Everyman in the morality play, who has to take stock at the end of his life and then make amends before passing into heaven. My Everyman is now watching a ball game. "Let's go, Dad," I say, grabbing hold of the oxygen tank.

"Where?"

"I'm taking you for a spin."

"Now? Why? My game is on."

"I didn't come all the way down here to watch TV."

"Can't we wait until the commercial?"

"As a matter of fact, we can't."

As much as I never wanted him in a wheelchair, there's

something almost enjoyable about the control over him it gives at this moment, enabling me to just move him along against his will. It satisfies me by putting the balance of power—always our struggle—on my side. With a lurch I push him out of his room and into the bright and empty hallway.

"Where should we go?" I ask.

"I don't know," he replies. "There's a lounge around the corner to the right."

We pass room after room with names next to doors. Some are closed, many open, giving me a peek at patients sitting up who look healthy, others who look at death's door. It makes me think of all the time spent with both my parents in hospitals, and all the sadness I've felt for them and sometimes desperation too, especially when my late mother's stays would go on for weeks, exposing her to all kinds of additional problems like staph infections and pneumonia. I don't know how people can sleep in places like this. I'm too much a control freak for the routines hospitals impose. Yet here I am imposing myself on my father.

We get to a small lounge looking out over a parking lot, where a big flat-screen TV plays in the dark. I turn it off but don't turn on any lights. I lock the brakes on my father's wheelchair and sit down on a leathery beige sofa to face him. He looks at me and shrugs. Light from the hallway hits half his face. The room is almost as small as a confessional.

"So, Dad, I was thinking about you."

"Always nice to hear that," he says.

"Have you been thinking about yourself?"

"What do you mean?"

Of course he's thinking about himself. Like me, it's his chief occupation. My methodical mother was the caregiver, always worrying about others. My brother is that way too, ready to jump in to do whatever it takes to make things work for our family. Not Dad or me. We're the ones to go for the fun and live in the moment without many plans. It works out at times, but other times not so much. Without plans, messes are made. But here, at the end of his life, I want to impose some order and narrate his ending as if it were a short story or fable.

"I mean you're getting to the…" and here I stutter. It's hard to say it. "To the end."

"I'd rather not talk about it," he says.

"But, Dad, it might make you feel better, I mean to talk about what you're thinking."

"Bobby, please, it just makes me uncomfortable."

I sigh. I sit back. He fiddles with his phone, then picks it up to make a call. It goes to voice mail and he leaves a message that's unusually short for a long-winded man.

"Doreen, it's me. Guess who I'm here with in the hospital? Bobby came down to visit and we're having a nice catch-up in the lounge! We hope you're enjoying the beautiful weather, and send our love to everyone. I'll be back at home tomorrow, so give me a call after nine p.m."

Nine p.m. is off-peak minutes. Part of me wants to lean in and snatch that little cell phone right out of his hands. It's shocking that even now he can annoy me by picking the thing up and using it while I'm in the room. I am, after all, doing my best to honor him with my full attention.

"So you don't feel like talking about big-picture stuff?" I ask.

"I don't know what you mean by that, but I'd be happy to hear what you've been doing all weekend and what your next column is going to be about."

He always likes hearing about what I'm writing for the paper. I'm not having any of it.

"I don't want to talk about what I'm writing about."

"Well, what, then?"

I think for a moment. This is the conundrum of familial love, isn't it? We can be there with the most important people in the world to us and have nothing to say to each other. I scan my head like a radio in the middle of nowhere without any stations coming in. Then I see the headline of a *USA Today* on a coffee table and it sets my head into something like battle mode.

"The war in Iraq isn't going so well," I say.

Dad lets off the sigh of an old steam engine. This isn't fair play, but it's the best I can do to keep the boredom away. I mean, here we are together with nobody around to amuse us. And Dad's been such a profound supporter of George Bush and his inane decision in the wake of 9/11 to go into

Iraq based on false information about nuclear weapons and Al Qaeda alliances. And of course Dad hasn't kept his opinions to himself. Rather, he's upended dinner parties, bridge games, and even one Passover Seder in defense of his beloved Republicans.

It's an embarrassment to me more than a real sore point. Dad has, after all, been nothing but humane when it comes to gay rights, women's issues, immigration, and social policy. He's really, as I often say, the world's most democratic Republican. But he's also stubborn. And now, even when the tide of public opinion has risen against the president and his administration, Dad goes on blindly blathering his support and haranguing all who argue. I find it regrettable and unacceptable. Is this my moment to help him see the light? I take a breath, let it out.

"So you still really think Bush is doing a good job?" I ask.

My tone is nonconfrontational. Dad, always quick to defend his views, stays quiet. He folds his hands in front of him as if at a Homeland Security interrogation. I lean in closer.

"You know, Dad, when you get near the end of your life, it's a time when you can reconsider things, take stock, say something you never would have said before."

He tilts his head to the side and looks at me, then sighs. Outside, there's an announcement ordering a nurse on the floor to report to intensive care.

"I'm not sure there's anything I'd want to say along those lines," he says.

I wait a moment. Like a hawk circling above, I have my eye on the kill.

"You know how we've always disagreed about politics?" I ask.

"I'd say we have always agreed to disagree, yes."

I'm quiet. I hear news about another suicide bombing in Iraq on a TV in the room next door. I hear two nurses say good night as an elevator door closes. Dad fishes a toothpick out of his shirt pocket and starts going at his teeth, making sucking noises and depositing food particles in a tissue he holds.

"Well, as a gesture toward some kind of closure, I have a proposal," I say.

"For what, Bobby?"

"Your redemption."

"What?"

"You know, the kind of thing you do near the end."

"Who said I'm at the end?"

"You, you've said it yourself over and over for the past twelve months."

"I don't mean to trouble you."

"But don't you think we're looking at something now that seems like the end?"

"What's this gesture toward my redemption that interests you so much?"

I clear my throat, sit back in my seat, and wait a moment before I answer.

"I would like you to renounce the Republican Party."

My father stays still. Then the hint of a smirk moves onto his face.

"You've got to be kidding," he says.

"No. Ralph scared the hell out of me and I drove down thinking this was it. I shlepped all the way here in the middle of a beautiful holiday weekend to say good-bye and here you are watching the game, hocking your cell phone service provider, and leaving chirpy messages to your girlfriend. I mean, I almost hit a deer and died on the road tonight."

"I should think you'd be happy to see me doing better than usual."

"I want to get my money's worth out of this trip, Dad."

He shakes his head and smirks again. I shouldn't be rattling him so much.

"Look, I appreciate your coming," he says. "I know you must have plans, and it's a long drive, especially in the dark. It really means the world to me that you're here, Bobby. It does."

There it is, that kindness, that gratitude that always disarms me, makes me regret every cynical thought, every disgruntled response I've lobbed at him my entire life. But I don't acknowledge it now or tell him it's my pleasure. Something is driving me on. I don't just want to have a collision with this beast that is his will. I want to take aim and shoot it, bring it down tonight and help him erase the mistakes of his past with one swift and potent renunciation.

"So I'm giving you a chance here, Dad. We don't have

to put anything in writing. I'm just asking you to tell me if you regret being such a staunch Republican your whole life."

He stops picking his teeth. He shakes his head with furrowed eyebrows. When he breathes out, it is so loud and long that it's as if his soul is leaving him, or part of it anyway.

"You're always pushing me, always trying to get me to see things your way. Why do you bother? You know how set I am in my ways. I know how set you are in yours."

I think about this for a moment. Why do I try to get him to change his views? I'm not him and he's not me. Shouldn't I be mature enough to know that?

"Dad, I'm just trying to seize the moment here."

"You really don't think I'm going to live much longer?"

"I mean I just want to ask, even if it's a little premature, will you consider, if only for me, renouncing the Republican Party? It could be an act of some kind of personal redemption."

He shakes his head and looks down into his lap. I am blushing now at my nerve and at my will. We could have had a nice visit without this confrontation. He looks me in the eye.

"I can say that I would not vote for George Bush again," he says.

"Really?"

"Yes."

I feel light pour into my brain as I hear it and see angels

reflected on his aviator glasses, circling the ceiling. My heart races but I don't say a word. I just let it sink in. He looks deflated. I feel for him and take his hand, bring it to my face, and kiss it as if it were the Pope's.

"You mean it?"

"Yes, I do," he says.

More angels, now with tennis racket wings and throwing a confetti of playing cards and bridge score sheets. Orchestras playing "Hava Nagila" and the national anthem. Judgment Day trumpets and klezmer clarinets. I feel such joy at his stunning capitulation.

"Well done, sir," I say. "Thank you very much."

"Well, you pushed me into it. What could I do?"

"But you're in your right mind and you do mean it?"

"Yes, I'm afraid I do. I would not vote for the present George Bush again."

I feel triumphant as I lean into him and feel his chest heaving against mine.

"Can I give you a hug?"

His eyebrows lift. He smiles. He is always open to any kind of affection.

"Sure."

I put my arms around his neck and, very careful to avoid the oxygen tubes, lean into his face, my big nose to his bigger one, and we hold ourselves there like teenagers in a slow dance.

"I love you, Dad," I say.

"I love you too, Bobby."

And then I get up, unlock his wheels, turn his chair around, find a remote control, turn the volume on the Mets game all the way up, and watch with him.

He takes my hand. We hold on to each other in the glow of the TV screen.

Spot of Light

It's the second Sunday in June and Dad's death is close now. The cardiac critical care floor at his local hospital seems quieter than other floors I've visited this year. Maybe it's because lives suddenly hang in the balance here, and people don't want to make noise. Cancer isn't so sudden, but when a heart seizes up and requires defibrillators, ventilators, and pumps to keep life going—it feels so precarious. My father is here after another siege. This one would have killed him if they hadn't gotten to him in time to put in a pump. We knew it was coming.

I've left Ira at the upstate house to drive down to Long Island again. My brother let me know, in his way, that dropping in sooner rather than later would be in everyone's best interest. He greets me in the hallway.

"I was almost going to tell you not to come," he says with a trace of apology and something else that is solemn and ominous. "But I wanted you to see this, talk to the doctors, get a sense of what's going on." I bristle for a moment at what I think of as his controlling things.

"I don't think I have anything to say to the doctors."

"I still wanted you to have the proper time to say good-bye."

It doesn't seem right to tell him I feel that I've already said good-bye. And it's hard to face the fact that once again, I'm thinking this way at the end of a parent's life. But just a few days ago my father and I had a nice evening that had a quiet finality and sense of closure. It was a dinner together in his building's dining room, where he made me laugh by making an outlandish concoction, adding cranberry juice to his tea. It's something he's done ever since I can remember, and ever since I can remember, I've winced at it. He stirred it with a shaky hand.

"Mad scientist," I told him. He winked and grinned. I bit my lip to keep from falling apart in front of him. I sensed I wouldn't be seeing him mix another concoction in this lifetime.

It's strange—not that long ago I was offended by his habits and table manners. I remember dreading having to deal with him with my mother out of the picture. Instead, this sweetness rose in us. He has become something like a friend, and also an indicator of what lies ahead for me. Ira points that out each time I pour orange juice into my red wine, leave monumental messes in the kitchen, or get into involved conversations with strangers when we're in a rush to get somewhere.

"I can't believe I married your father," he says with both affection and alarm.

After our final dinner together, Dad and I retired to the piano in his lobby, which was quiet, and although he was weak, we made it through Rodgers and Hammerstein's "You'll Never Walk Alone," with its rising chords that strain as if to lift a tired soul straight up to the red-carpet arrival zone of heaven. As a last song it seemed better than any final words between us. His struggle was ending, and the satisfaction of his final release would be coming soon. We didn't have to talk about it. He was so weak that we both knew it. We just knew.

His room in the critical care unit is a white box without windows. His eyes are closed, his forehead smooth as always, his hair sugar white and silky straight, but he looks worn out in a way that has never showed on his face until now. A big blue corrugated tube that almost looks like a hose leads from a bedside machine to underneath his white blanket. It's the pump for his heart that's keeping him alive. It's clear he won't be leaving this bed.

Jeff has to get back to the city. He has an office to run and a date with his son and apologizes for not staying longer. "Of course, of course," Dad tells him. "I don't want you to have to trouble yourself any more than necessary, either of you. You know that."

I wish Jeff could stay. I don't want to be left alone here. I'm scared that something will go wrong. But that isn't likely when a pump is in a heart to keep it going. It's a kind of life support that doesn't malfunction. Jeff leaves and it's just Dad and me now.

"So, Bobby, how was the weekend?" he asks.

What to say? Except for my obsession with the brown river and also the plague of tent caterpillars defoliating the mountainsides, it was a lovely weekend with Ira, early summer in the mountains. That's not to say that even the loveliest of times don't have an edge for me. For the last ten years or more, any happiness, any trip to a sweet place has been darkened by thoughts about the suffering of one of my parents.

"It was nice," I tell him now. "It's a pretty time of year upstate."

"Strawberry season," he says.

"Yes," I say, "strawberry season."

We talk as much as he's able. He's half distracted by a ball game, but not as much as usual. Perhaps it means less to him, knowing he won't be around for any play-offs this fall. He reaches for my hand and I hold it. It is shaped just like mine, with the same straight small thumb and wisps of hair on the knuckles. I fill the time with chatter. He listens but doesn't respond.

A nurse comes in to tend the machines, the drips, the indicators of pulse and breathing, and I watch him rally as he always does around strangers.

"Lily, I want to introduce you to my younger son," he says.

The nurse turns to shake my hand. "Nice to meet you," she says.

"He's the writer," my father adds. "What are you working on right now, Bob?"

The question, as always, makes me cringe at having to be his dancing poodle. I know I should answer him but don't. I have to hand something in to my editor on Thursday, a few days away. It might be about my first Father's Day without him.

"And how's the show going?" he asks.

The show about his dating year, which now seems such ancient history, has been a big disappointment. I'm no draw, and the subject of my father dating after my mother died isn't sexy enough to make a mark, and for any number of reasons that keep me up at night, it has been impossible to get an audience, even one night a week in a tiny space. He never thought the show would amount to much.

"It's doing okay," I say. "I have a couple more nights and then it's over."

"Maybe something will happen for you," he says.

"Maybe it will."

"You never know."

I don't remind him how, not all that long ago, he laid a curse on my ambitions beyond journalism and told me that my pursuit of show business would likely lead to nothing. Why bring that into the room when his mortality is weighing down on both of us now? Why hold on to resentment?

"You're right, Dad," I say. "You never know."

Time in a hospital, even at a dire end time like this one, can slacken. The hour ahead of visiting seems to stretch out like a marathon drive or late-night shift.

"Late?" he says at some point.

"Yes," I say. "I guess I should go."

"Bobby," he says as he squeezes my hand. "Thank you."

"I'll see you tomorrow," I say.

"I love you," he says. "You've been a wonderful son."

Is he thinking, like me, that this is a last good-bye? It might not be, since he's on life support. But maybe it's not such a bad thing to treat each good-bye as if it's a last one. It gives resonance to the moment, puts us on our best behavior, removes the pettiness and adds the meaning so that we really see each other, hear each other, feel what is so sacred in our time together. Is this the moment to thank him for everything? For knowing how to be a father when he grew up an orphan himself? For showing such interest and for always letting me know that he's thrilled to see me, even when I let him know I want to be elsewhere?

"No, Dad, it's me who should be thanking you," I say. "You've been so..."

He holds up his hand. Then a stiff smile crosses his face.

Maybe he isn't ready for this forced finality. Or does he want to have these last moments without any words at all?

"You don't want to talk anymore?" I ask.

"I'm having a bowel movement," he whispers.

I have to laugh. It's just so Dad. Then I call for the nurse. Time to go.

That night at home I wonder how long he will linger with that pump in his heart. I know he doesn't want to live, but it will be awkward bringing it up with the hospital staff. The magic words "comfort care" or "palliative care" can help them understand that he doesn't want to fight anymore. But he needs to tell them himself. It's on his health proxy—DNR, do not resuscitate. But that's not what good-hearted medical technicians think about at emergency scenes. They aim to save lives, not save patients from having to live them.

When I arrive back at his room the following day, my brother is with him and talking to a doctor by the side of the bed. As usual, I feel marginalized. But then, I'm the one who arrives late. My brother introduces me to the doctor. "I'll leave you to discuss things," he says.

I turn to Jeff. "What things?"

"We've been talking about the options," he says.

"Options? Meaning what?"

"Look, Bobby, I really don't want to draw this out longer than necessary," Dad says.

I'm glad to hear him say it aloud. I've been thinking about it for so long, his final advance toward a sanctioned release. We both have.

"He wants to be removed from the pump," Jeff says.

"And what will that do? What happens then?" I ask.

"The doctor is suggesting that his heart will eventually stop. And with a morphine drip to ease the discomfort and the pain, he won't feel anything. He'll just drift and fall asleep."

"Just what I wanted, just as I'd imagined," Dad says with something like cheer.

I nod. We all nod together as the machines at his bed blink and beep.

I'm relieved there's no conflict, the way there was with our mother. And I'm so grateful that Jeff has taken the lead to open the conversation. But then, with my father he doesn't have the urge to hold on to him a moment longer. It is just so clear that the old man has wanted to go.

Dad clears his throat as if he were about to present a case in court.

"I don't want any more life support. I want to just go to sleep and be done with all this now, period." There's a nonnegotiable tone in his voice that's even more unyielding than when he's miffed at his cell phone service provider or a clueless bridge partner. Jeff and I exchange looks, nod again.

Not that any of us would argue. There's no question now, no fear, and no shaming accusations lobbed at me for wanting to end things for my own convenience. Equanimity floods in. Dad's ready. And we are too. "How soon do you want the pump out, Dad?" I ask.

"I already said as soon as possible, whenever the staff can do it."

"You mean today?" Jeff asks.

I think, *No, not today, because it could mean staying up all night waiting for him to expire. That would mean I'd have to cancel my show tonight. That would mean I wouldn't have enough time to write my column, due Thursday.*

"What about tomorrow?" Dad asks. "It would give me time to make some calls."

"Are you sure that's good for you, Dad?" Jeff asks.

He nods once. "Why should I wait?"

Indeed, why should he? He doesn't want any visitors, doesn't have any final business to tie up, and he's lost all interest in TV. He's bored, uncomfortable, and ready to shut down for good. It appears to be as simple for him as an employee deciding to give notice.

"The doctor says that once they pull the pump, it'll be half a day or so," Jeff says. "So why don't we let you give it some thought and then let us know what you think?"

I look at Jeff. *Why does he have to give it some thought?*

"Boys, I'm telling you that I want to be gone by tomorrow night, that's that," Dad says.

Jeff and I look at each other. Then we nod in agreement.

"Please," he says. Then he closes his eyes to rest.

Out in the hallway later, on a floor that's all about saving lives by whatever means are necessary, not letting them slip away, we talk it through some more and I'm relieved we are in easy agreement. "I'm glad we can let him have what he wants," Jeff says.

I don't want to bring up my show tonight because I'm ashamed to admit it's something I'm thinking about. How could anyone be fixated on getting up to perform, seduce an audience, when a loved one's life is ending? Is my need for attention so great that I can't give it a rest, call off the show? It's not as if there's money involved or that anyone would care if I canceled, given how small the box office has been. And of course it's all the more complicated and convoluted because the subject of the show is Dad in all his vital and eccentric glory. Jeff, always thinking for everyone, gets to it first and saves me from having to skirt the question.

"What about your performance tonight?" he asks.

"I guess I could cancel it," I say.

"But aren't there people coming?"

"Not many, a couple dozen maybe."

"Don't cancel it. Dad wouldn't want that."

I look at my feet and nod. I'm grateful. Jeff has released me from the guilt that would have come with rushing off this afternoon to dress and get to the theater on time, and has given me his approval to go off and do what he knows I do best—take care of myself by amusing others. It's a paradox I live with as his younger brother, seeking his approval while seething about his need to give it. But is there something in his judging that I need to keep me from making the worst choices, ones I will regret and that will haunt me all my life? I would not have wanted to live without him during these difficult times with our parents. And I know it isn't just his approval that I need. It's him, his wit, generosity, fierce protectiveness, and how he cares for all of us.

"I guess I should get going," I say.

"Break a leg," Jeff says. "I hope you have a wonderful show."

It's a terrible show, of course. When I walk onstage in the basement cabaret, I see there's a smaller audience than I had thought. While a bartender dumps ice in the back of the tiny space, the pianist pounds away on an upright as I pound away at the material as if on autopilot. I don't want to feel anything as I talk about my father tonight because if I do, I'll fall apart. My hands are clammy, my vision a little blurred from the small halogen stage lights aimed at my forehead. This is so intimate, I might as well be performing in our living room, the way I did as a child, when Dad would sit on the couch with Mom and applaud and sing along with unbridled delight. At elementary and junior high concerts I couldn't see him from the back of the band, where I was playing baritone horn. When I sang in the chorus, I'd scan the audience until I'd find him out there. He never missed a concert, not even for tennis, and he never missed the chance to record them on his funky cassette recorder.

Years later, in my early forties, when I was living in the Hamptons in the summer, single and out of sorts, my parents would drive out each Tuesday night from their unglamorous suburb to hear me play trombone with the Sag Harbor Community Band. I never knew what to do with them when they'd visit. I didn't want to scare them with the prices at expensive restaurants or introduce them to the few friends I had. They didn't fit the upscale image I wanted to convey. Of course I was angry with myself for feeling this way, a grown man with the status issues of a teenager. But with the band, we found common ground.

My father thought we sounded wonderful, even when we didn't. "It's nice to see all those years of music lessons pay off," my mother would say. She was very fragile at the time, and it took some effort for her to get out of their car and hobble to sit down on the lawn chairs my father had set up with the small crowd in front of the American Legion post. At our first concert of the summer of 2001, I watched them arrive from behind my music stand, where I was putting my sheet music in order. Then we played our Sousa marches and show tunes. I was nervous but did pretty well with "Some Enchanted Evening."

"Way to go, Bob," our conductor said.

The real enchantment of the evening came later, when we played "New York, New York." At some point I looked up at the crowd. There, under a rising half-moon, my parents were dancing, holding each other close against the winds of change that were aging them so quickly. It threw me back to when they were a handsome young couple and I would sit on the stairs in my pajamas and look at them in the living room, dancing to cha-cha records late at night. How could they ever have been so young? And how could they get so old before my eyes? We were playing "Getting to Know You," and my father was standing up and singing. And as I strained to play for them just as I had at all those school concerts, I could see that our music was making them young again and it was doing the same for me. The sunset faded, the stars came out above Sag Harbor's marina, with masts ringing in the summer wind.

I wish they could be out there in my audience tonight, egging me on and helping me get through this show. But my mother is gone and my father's been too weak to come to any performances this year. He saw an early version of the show, when I had hope for it. It wasn't easy material for him—being depicted as a man ready to hunt down new love within months of the death of his wife of fifty years. But when I saw him embracing my friends afterward with his lime-green sweater tied around his neck, I was both proud and grateful.

I spiel to my audience about his annoying habits and hilarious outbursts. He's great material, always has been, a man who taught me not to be afraid to sing and not to be crippled by dignity, a father and a muse. Is there time to thank him for that before he passes away tomorrow?

At home that night, with Ira, the other love of my life, holding me in bed, I cry and can't stop, unable to find my way to sleep.

"By tomorrow night he'll be gone," I say.

"You've been a good son," Ira says.

If only I could believe that.

It's busy in his room the next morning. Nurses are hovering, and so are my aunt Bev and her daughter Randy, who brought yogurt-coated raisins and pita chips, which we munch as if we're watching a movie. Ralph, my father's aide, is here too, and is watching a talk show on TV. I know their intentions are excellent—they all love my father and want to do the right thing by being supportive—but I don't want them around. This is to be my father's last day on the earth, and it seems that what he wants now is quiet, nothing more.

Eventually, when Jeff and I are left alone with him, a nurse comes in. She speaks to us softly. Since my father made his decision to move from a critical care scenario to one of hospice and departure, the staff has become even kinder and more comforting. "If everyone's okay, we'll get ready to remove the pump," the nurse says. Her tone is so gentle that it softens the shock as she asks us to leave the room because of the intensity of the procedure. We tell Dad good-bye and that we'll be back in a while, knowing everything will be changed for him when we return.

He tells us to take our time. "I'm not going anywhere too fast," he says.

When we come back the pump is gone. The nurse is smiling, Dad is napping.

"I have to tell you what happened when we pulled it out," she says. "He sat up in bed for the first time since Sunday and his arms shot up into the air and he shouted 'Wonderful!' It was incredible—we'd never seen anything like that before." It made us smile. My father always knew how to charm the staff at hospitals. Which is why it surprises us when a middle-aged man in a dark suit, a rabbi, steps into the room holding a prayer book and Dad doesn't greet him.

"May I come in and talk to your father?" he asks us.

It seems like a good idea, something final and ritualistic to help pass the time.

"Dad," my brother says, "would you like the rabbi to come in?"

My father shakes his head, still very present and relaxed as if on a chaise lounge by a pool. He seems to be enjoying the first phase of the ride to his sweet and long-awaited oblivion.

"No rabbi for me," he says. "It's not necessary."

The rabbi looks a little surprised—but no more so than any number of people my father has surprised his whole life—and he nods and leaves us. But my brother, the more devout of the two of us and perhaps thinking about our mother, looks uncomfortable. He glances over at me for support, but I have none to give. My father's wishes are all that matter to me right now. I fought with Dad his whole life over little things. Not today.

"What would be the harm with a blessing or two?" Jeff asks him.

"Please, I really don't need it," he replies.

"He's fine, Jeff," I add. "Let it be, let him have it his way now."

It's no surprise he doesn't want religion. Once our mother was gone, all bets were off in terms of faith. While my brother went to services for the year after her death to say Kaddish, the mourner's prayer, Dad and I didn't keep up with it for long. Dad stopped worrying about attending synagogue on the High Holidays too, and ramped up the eating of seafood and pork. He said he'd lost any faith he had in God after watching his wife suffer for so long. My brother understood this and even sanctioned his choice to go AWOL from Judaism after his devout wife died. Yet something in Jeff makes him go out into the hall, retrieve the rabbi, and bring him back to the room. I feel my pulse start racing.

"It'll only take a minute, Dad," he says.

My father doesn't have the strength to object and I don't have the nerve. But I am uncomfortable. How can my brother force this rabbi on a man who said he doesn't want him here? Where is his respect for last wishes? Is he doing this for his own needs? Or is it for our whole family, and something that a good son does to sanctify transition and passing? The rabbi opens his book. He is soft-spoken and soothing as he reads from a confessional end-of-life prayer about missing the world and separating from loved ones.

When he finishes, the rabbi takes a seat at our father's side.

"So now I'm going to talk to you a few more minutes, Mr. Morris, then I'll leave you alone," he says. "I'll just tell you a few things that might be of interest. Is that okay?"

Dad opens his eyes to look over at the rabbi, and he nods.

"Some like to suggest at times like this to think about a spot that's inside you, inside all of us, when we're born, which is a little bit of God. It grows as you become a good son and a good parent and it grows even more each time you do a good deed in life, each time you listen, each time you help someone. It's a record of your achievements and the love you've shown throughout your life. And being with you now, today, Mr. Morris, near the end of your life, all I have to do is look at you and your two sons who love you so much and I can imagine that by now that spot of God in you is pretty big."

Dad nods almost imperceptibly.

"One more thought, if I may, Mr. Morris," the rabbi says. "Dad nods again. "Call me Joe," he whispers.

"I want you to imagine your whole life now if you can, Joe," the rabbi says as my brother and I lean in. "And for each time you did something good, I mean something that helped someone, regardless of how small, imagine it as a little glow, a little spot of illumination that lights a long dark roadway. So if you look back behind you at your whole life now, I imagine you can see many, many lights glowing there, stretching back to the horizon."

My father nods again, and so do I. It's a lovely talk. Through my tears, I can see those spots of light, *his* spots of light, glowing as if in a mist of years as they trail off into the darkness: the desserts he brought to delight my mother, the pride he had in me, the games he played on his hands and knees with nieces and grandchildren, the tennis balls he gave to kids in parks, the postcards he sent to lonely neighbors, the concern he showed fragile relatives and how he made them feel welcome, including my grandfather, whom he invited into our home for the last ten years of life. The pro bono law work. The friendliness to strangers, a kind of grace.

Yes, the lights are there, glowing pearly white as they trail back into darkness. He's done the best he can for his whole lifetime. Like me. Like my brother, all of us. The best we can.

When the rabbi finishes, he gets up and pats Dad's arm.

Dad holds on to his hand. "Rabbi, that was just beautiful," he says.

The rabbi looks pleased and asks if he can hug us. Jeff and I aren't huggers, in fact it's almost a joke between us—how little we like to be touched, let alone kissed or caressed. But we allow the rabbi to put his arms around us and we feel his embrace.

"Thank you so much," Jeff says.

"Yes, thank you so much," I echo.

I'm not sure what to think except that Jeff was right to bring him in.

Time passes, the morphine drips. My father's breathing becomes a little softer.

Jeff does a crossword puzzle. I read a magazine. Nurses look in now without saying a word. There's nothing more to be done. Once in a while, my father opens his eyes for a moment and smiles at us as if through a happy haze.

"Still here," I say.

"Thank you, boys," he says.

A little later, Jeff takes a container from a plastic bag. "Hey, Dad, I have some strawberries. Do you want one?" Dad doesn't reply. He seems to be shaking his head. Or is he moving his lips? Jeff approaches him and sits down at his side.

"I don't think he wants anything anymore," I say.

"But he loves strawberries," Jeff says. "Don't you, Dad?"

In fact, he got great pleasure from his little backyard patch of them, and also the raspberries that he grew just a stone's throw from the septic tank in our small suburban plot. He was no friend of nature, no trail or beach could lure him from his air-conditioned car, but he loved his little backyard garden and would come inside to us, delighted with a small candy dish full of his beloved berries. In the kitchen, he'd hand them to our mother, who would coo.

"Wow, they're gorgeous, Joe," she'd say. And then they would kiss on the lips.

My brother steps up to the side of the bed now, strawberries ready. He raises one to my father's lips and I step back from the bed to keep myself from pushing it away. But my father leans forward to take it into his mouth. He doesn't choke on it. Rather, he chews it slowly and then, with a gulp-like swallow loud enough to surprise us, it's gone. A spot of red juice remains on his bottom lip. He licks it off. Jeff picks another strawberry from his box, one shaped like a heart. I feel my hands claw my legs and my jaw clench. I resent this intrusion.

"Isn't that good, Dad?" he says. "Do you want another?"

He does not. But I detect a smile on his slack face. We both do.

A few minutes later, when we're outside and the shadows of the hospital are creeping over a garden where we sit, I can't stop seething. How dare my brother impose on my father's last wishes? I have no motivation at his deathbed now other than to help him go as he wants. Or do I?

Maybe I'm the one imposing too much by not letting Jeff say good-bye in his own way. The whole thing feels so Jacob and Esau—brothers in conflict at a father's deathbed.

"Strawberries, Jeff? Why? Can't you see he wants to be left to drift away now?"

"I just wanted to give him a little sensory reminder of what he loves," he says.

"Why? Why would you do that when all he wants to do is sleep?"

I don't understand my rage. All Jeff wants to do is help make a lovely ending. But it bothers me that it's *his* ending, and not the one our father is stipulating.

We sit on a bench, drinking hospital coffee in the late-afternoon light, the same time of day when we sat together drinking coffee four years ago outside the hospital where our mother was dying. Our conflict then was more profound because we disagreed about her wishes. Today we both know, ultimately, what our father wants. We just didn't imagine it so soon.

"So are you telling me you want me feeding you things on your deathbed?"

"Yes, I am," Jeff says. "If you're there."

Is he saying he can't count on me to be there if he is the first to die? I can't say I blame him, after he had to force me home for our mother. I've missed many key moments in his life.

I push the thought away. Then I pull it back in and hold it close, breathe it in.

Of course I will be there. I want to be there. I have to be.

"Okay, Jeff, so you want me to bring you something to eat on your deathbed?"

"If it's not too inconvenient for you, yes."

I finish my coffee and slam-dunk it into a trash can and turn and face him.

"So tell me, what is it that you want? What sensory reminder of the world is it that you want to smell and taste as you are drifting off into the great abyss?"

It takes him about half a second to answer me and he leans in to do it.

"Butterscotch ice cream."

We stare at each other. Our minds meld and melt to remember scenes of childhood and tubs of generic supermarket ice milk in a suburban kitchen where our mother served us with the family cat underfoot.

Then we laugh until the tears come.

"You better watch out I don't put it on your nose," I say.

Hours later, back in the windowless white room, which feels as protected from the world as a womb, my brother looks up from his newspaper at my father, whose breath is light and soft now, a hint of breathing, nothing more. Jeff has one more thing he needs to do, and he walks over to the CD player he brought out from the city, the same one he brought to my mother's hospital bed. "How about some music, Dad?" he says.

"No, no music," my father manages to reply.

I'm surprised, but I understand. I can see on his face that he's enjoying the drifting out, leaving us without pain, without worry or concern, detaching from the world.

"What about if we sing you a couple of favorites?" my brother asks.

"Please," Dad says with something like urgency, "no more singing."

This, from a man who sang his way through life, is something new to us. It says so definitively that he is through.

"Let's just do a couple of songs for him," Jeff says.

I can't believe my ears. I can't believe the presumption.

"But he just told us no singing," I say.

"What about 'You Are My Sunshine'?"

"But he just said he doesn't want it."

"Please, let's just do it for him anyway."

Jeff looks both vulnerable and intent. I do understand his need, as I understood how we all wanted to sing for my mother. We'll never know if she heard our Sabbath prayers or those songs we sang together on her last night. But we could not have known, because she couldn't communicate her wishes. So we did our things, had our rituals, and while we believed we were singing for her, we must have known whom we were really singing for—each other. It is impossible to understand until you are in the room with someone like my brother, who clings so hard to the lives he loves that death is for the living, just as much as life is. We need to make it our own, to do what we feel is the best last thing.

And as I realize that, with my brother by my side, a man who has done nothing but protect me, shower gifts on me all his life, and share his life with me as if I were his own son, I open my mouth, and in the sweetest tone I can summon to break the sacred quiet, I sing with him.

> *You'll never know, dear*
> *How much I love you . . .*

When we finish, I notice that our father is nodding. He must have enjoyed it. Of course he did.

More time passes. And when I look up at him again from my magazine, his breathing is even slower, markedly lighter, as if he needs only the tiniest trace of air now to go on. Another hour passes, maybe more. And then it happens—there is no breath to follow his last. His heart has stopped and his face is still, eyes and mouth closed in repose. His hand starts to get cooler. I let go of it, but we stay in our chairs for a while longer, taking in what has happened. We have no parents now, nobody to love us in the way they did, nobody to love as we loved them. And we also have no worries now, no concerns for a suffering so close that it often felt like our own.

Then, whoosh, thoughts about life rush in like waves. Should I go right home to my desk and e-mail my editor that I want to file a column to run on Father's Day? Or do I tell him my father just died and that I don't want to file, even though I do? Should I cancel the show next Monday, the last, or go through with it, with him gone less than a week? And how to begin arranging the graveside service he requested a year ago in his suicide letter? How to begin after his end?

Life floods back into my head with all its practicalities. But my brother stays still in his chair, still staring at my father, a man who aggravated him and disappointed him so much when it came to caring for our mother in her last years. He didn't provide her with the care Jeff wanted. He didn't love her in the most responsible way.

"Should we get going?" I ask.

"Just another minute," he says.

I don't want to stay another minute, but I do. I have to force myself to, just as I have to force myself to see us in this new life—as siblings without parents. "Orphans" seems too strong a word—we aren't young and impoverished or oppressed. Although certainly our lives will be poorer now without the two people who were so elemental to us.

I once heard someone say that after birth, parents are a luxury. He said it because his parents were so terrible that he had to learn to live his life without relying on them for anything. He said that if you have one good parent, you're extremely lucky, and that if you have two, you've won the lottery. I think that if you can add to that a brother who cares so much, even as he guilt-trips you into being the best son you can be, there's nothing more to want from a family.

He sits there for so long it makes me feel a restlessness that turns to resentment. And of course I feel conflicted about the resentment. Then I feel angry with myself. Nothing changes,

I guess. I imagine I will feel this way for years, always with regret. But then I imagine something else—*not feeling this way*. Is it possible that we have a future ahead of us when we will be able to rest easy, knowing we each did our best as sons, each in the way that we could?

I don't know. But as I sit with Jeff looking at our father's still body, I remember sitting with him four years ago when he would not leave our mother for an hour after she died. I remember how he wanted to engage with her in her last hours, the Sabbath, through her dying process, and I think about all the rituals he insisted on having in the presence of our father today. Yes, death is for the living—to embrace and make our own. And if we are very lucky, we are present when the same people who gave us our first breaths breathe their last ones.

Time passes. Jeff finally gets up, collects his CD player and strawberries. Soon, with arms around each other, we are walking through the hospital hallway, passing families still struggling to get well, hold on, stay strong. All that is over for us now. We step outside into the dazzling brightness of June. I feel sad, and also lighter than I've felt in many years.

Dad and Cousin Julie

Speech

An hour or so after our father is gone, I'm in Jeff's car and we're leaving Long Island to drive back to the city. We are not yet used to life without parents. It will take a long time to get there—deleting numbers from contact lists and realizing we no longer have the two most important people to call with good news or birthday wishes. Jeff has kids. I don't and I already am starting to feel weightless. Thank goodness I have Ira.

"It was easier than with Mom," Jeff says.

"Yeah, well, Dad wanted out," I reply.

Sadness and relief mingle around us. We listen to music. We discuss the funeral—simple and graveside at Dad's request. We are getting on the expressway when my phone rings. It's my cousin Julie, a few years younger than me, a devoted niece to my dad. We're close.

"I just heard and I'm so sorry," she says. "I wanted to be there to say good-bye, but I've been in too much pain to get off my back and into the car. Now I wish I'd forced myself."

She's been losing her struggle with breast cancer.

"It's okay, sweetheart, he didn't want visitors, so you shouldn't feel bad," I assure her.

"No, he wanted to see me, I know it," she says. "I loved him so much."

They did love each other. Until he gave up on life in his last year, he had been an unusually loving uncle, and so the loss is profound to her. But her emotional response is already making me uncomfortable. Why does she need to be more consoled than me about his death?

"Don't cry," I tell her. "He was ready to go—you know that, we all did."

I guess I'm already divesting myself of him. But then, when someone is so weak and depressed for so long, you mourn the loss long before the actual demise. The fun-loving father and uncle we knew died a year ago. I tell Julie what the nurse reported about his ecstatic response—"Wonderful!"—to having his pump pulled out. She loves hearing it.

"I just wish he could have lived until Nicole's Bat Mitzvah," she says.

Nicole is her daughter, a popular kid on her school dance team. Her Bat Mitzvah in a couple of weeks is to be a Long Island bacchanal to rival any showstopper wedding.

"He really didn't want to see anyone, especially at a party," I say.

"I was going to get him to come, but now it's too late."

She breaks down into more sobs that rise and fall. Who knew she even had the strength for such grief? She is so frail and sallow these days, like a marsh reed in winter.

"He and I were soul mates in so many ways," she sighs.

Indeed, she is as open and unafraid to speak her mind as he was. And like him, she has a lovely voice and an endearing way of breaking into song at any moment. I remember her singing at our living room piano—an awkward, dark-haired girl in pigtails with an ethereal voice. She sang show tunes with my father—the Judy Garland ingenue alongside the crooning, swarthy romantic in a cardigan. She has maintained the lilt and loveliness through years of illness. She was ecstatic to meet Ira and know that I'd finally found a life partner. She called it *beshert*, Yiddish for a match between soul mates that is meant to be. With the enthusiasm of a true seeker, she has read every New Age book about health and healing. As my brother steers us onto the Triborough Bridge, and the logistics and challenges of city life start to press in, Julie is telling me about understanding my father's despair. She talks about souls leaving bodies, as his has done today. She says she could even sense when it was happening. For a lawyer and mother of two, she sounds way out there.

"I'm sensitive to energy," she says. "I knew the moment he passed away."

She's more attuned to everything now, she tells me. Who can blame her for thinking this way? The cancer is taking her down, but she is doing her best to find meaning in her suffering. It's something she wants to share with the world—the meaning—no matter how difficult it gets.

"I want to speak at his funeral," she declares. "There are things I want to say."

My head drops. I sigh and shift in my car seat and shoot my brother a look. She doesn't seem capable of speaking lucidly in her condition. And the last thing I want is for her to make an embarrassing scene, New Age or otherwise, at my father's grave.

"But do you think you can make it to the cemetery?"

"Look, I know I have to get there, and I will."

"You'll have to walk to the grave from the road. It's not close."

"I have a cane. It's not much worse than getting to the couch from my bedroom."

"And then you'll have to stand for the whole service."

"I'll bring a beach chair. You can just tell me when it's my turn to speak."

How can I tell her that I don't want her to? She has so much she wants to say. It has become an important part of what she has been calling her journey. I was visiting her in the hospital last winter when she told me about her personal mandate to be of more service.

"I try to make a difference when I see people in pain," she was saying.

Her hair had grown back from the latest round of chemo, but her skin was jaundiced from other complications. With the fragility of an ailing octogenarian, she got herself up from her bed. Her lips pressed together to keep from wincing in pain. Her eyes squinted. Even if it was a strain, she wanted to take a stroll. She wanted to keep using her body so it wouldn't shut down.

"Let me help you," I said.

"No, I want to do it," she replied between steps. "I'm fine."

We got to an empty lounge that looked out over the East River and beyond to Long Island, where her children and husband were far away and going about the week without her.

"It's more restful for me in a hospital in the city," she said. "I'm free to be sick."

"I never thought about it that way."

"I'm trying to stay positive."

"You're amazing." It was true. She had not become bitter at all. She took my hand. The light from the window made her glow golden. Suddenly she looked beautiful.

"I have to tell you about what I did last weekend," she said, breaking into a smile. She used her hand to move her legs in her chair; then she sat back, adjusting her gown.

"On Friday I drove Nicole to a dance competition in Jersey," she said. "And after three hours on the road, my back was killing me. So when we got there, I found a quiet corner near the stage where nobody could see me, and I lay down flat out on my back on the floor."

That was when she heard fighting from inside a nearby doorway:

"I'm not going on! She can't talk to me like that!"

"She's been your coach for years. She didn't mean anything."

"She did so, she meant every word! I'm not going on!"

"But everyone is waiting for you. You're the star!"

From her place on the floor, Julie sat up to see a girl named Mary, the best student in her daughter's dance school, fighting with her mother. Julie steadied herself against a chair, took a breath, and got herself up on her feet to go to the girl as her mother was storming away. Her number was starting in ten minutes. Julie went and stood over her like a suburban prophet.

"Excuse me," she whispered. "May I talk to you for a moment?"

The girl looked down, shook her head, and tossed her hair back.

"You might not know me, but I'm Nicole's mom," Julie said.

The girl nodded but then looked away as if she didn't understand English.

"And I know who you are. You're Mary, and I've been watching you for years. You're such a great dancer, and Nicole talks about you all the time. She wants to be like you. Everyone does in your school."

"That's not true," the girl muttered. "How do you know that?"

"Isn't it obvious, Mary? I'm sure you hear it all the time. You're fabulous."

As Julie went on with the story, she sat up straighter in the hospital lounge. A smile on her face was erasing some of the illness and worry. She said she looked the girl straight in the eye and held her gaze as the dance competition went on nearby. "Now, I don't know what happened in there with your coach," she told me she had said. "I don't really care. I don't even care if you go out there in ten minutes to dance. But I want you to ask yourself what you think it will be like a year from now when this competition is over and you're on to other things. Ask yourself how you want to remember today. Fighting with your coach? Or fighting for your team to win? It's up to you how you want to use your time here, Mary, you and nobody else."

Then Julie patted her shoulder and stood back.

"The choice is yours, all yours."

The girl wiped her eyes, Julie said. Then, like some kind of phoenix rising from the ashes, she stood up, brushed herself off, threw back her hair, and hustled to her dressing room, where Julie could hear her calling out for her costume. Then she went on.

"I still can't believe I did that," Julie told me.

"Did you ever tell Nicole about it?" I asked.

"Yes, and I'm sure she was mortified," Julie said.

But never mind. Julie wanted to be of service in a world that didn't want to look at her.

Now, months later, here I am, riding home in my brother's car a few hours after our father has died, worrying that she will embarrass us at his funeral. Is it that I'm ashamed of her too for looking so close to death and that I don't want her imposing? Is that why we don't let ourselves spend the time we should looking at the sick and the dying around us? My brother merges onto the FDR Drive. Traffic is mercifully light. We have no time to waste. He and I have calls and arrangements to make. I have to get Julie off the phone. She is weeping again.

"He was a wonderful uncle," she says.

"And you were a wonderful niece."

Soon after, I am telling her good-bye, clicking off, and looking at my brother.

"Shit," I say. "She wants to make a speech."

He looks at me, then back at the road. Here is something he knows he can't control.

"Well, there's nothing you can do about it now," he says.

"No?" I ask.

The next day, a new rabbi from our old family synagogue calls to ask about our father. She doesn't know him and is preparing a eulogy. I choke up telling her about his love of puns, song parodies, and his fifty-year marriage, which was a constant process for our mother of cleaning up the messes he loved making. I tell the rabbi how he loved to sing, and that he used to croon Frank Sinatra's "All the Way" in the kitchen while dancing with Mom. The rabbi says she'll find the lyrics. Then I suggest she call my cousin Julie. I admit to her that I'm worried (as is Julie's mother) about her speech. Would the rabbi talk to her, incorporate her observations in her eulogy, and credit her for them? Maybe it will satisfy Julie's need to bare her soul at the cemetery.

"I'll try," the rabbi says.

*   *   *

The day of the funeral, my brother and I arrive late from the city, true to the spirit of a father who often kept us waiting for him as children. The rabbi pins black ripped pieces of fabric on our lapels to symbolize mourning. She reports that Julie has told her that she will, in fact, be speaking. She also tells us that a man we don't know wants to sing. He's the new boyfriend of a friend of our parents and has a song for funerals.

"What song? Who is he?" I ask.

"His name is Ron, that's all I know," the rabbi says.

"He wrote a song for our father?" I ask.

"Did he even meet our father?" my brother asks.

"What is he, the funeral singer?" Ira asks.

Jeff and I smile. The rabbi shrugs. People smother us with hugs. Some cry. I don't feel like getting emotional. After crying about him for the past few days, I now just feel relief that he got his wish to die. Or maybe my stoicism is about control. He was so uncontrollable his whole life. I want this funeral to be short and dignified, not a rambling mess.

It's a clear June day, and good weather for a mourning procession. At the grave, freshly dug and dusty, the rabbi welcomes us and says a prayer. Then the man named Ron steps up to sing. He wears something that looks like a leisure suit. "We will remember him," he sings over and over in a bold baritone as my brother and his wife and Ira and I exchange looks that indicate something between amusement and mortification, much the same as the looks we often exchanged around my unchecked father.

The rabbi's eulogy is appropriate but somewhat unsatisfying because she never knew him. And how can anyone capture a man as iconoclastic as he was? After apologizing for not really knowing the tune, she pulls out the lyrics to "All the Way" and clears her throat.

"When somebody needs you, it's no good unless he needs you," she sings.

Her grasp of the tune is tentative and her voice strained. Much as it is coming from the right place, a wonderful, giving, and vulnerable place, it sounds all wrong. Each line of the song goes further off-key and away from the beautiful melody I still hear in my head the way our father sang it to our mother. I feel myself becoming agitated. Then I get so upset that I find myself starting to step forward to interrupt, take over, and sing the song myself.

But then I look at the rabbi's flushed face, with the same eyebrows arched upward as my father when he sang. She is lost in song just as he used to be, just as I often am. And she is trying her best to put something lovely into the world. I breathe and step back, and then I lean against the magnolia tree behind me to still myself. I tell myself to let it go.

"What's the harm?" my father might have asked.

When Julie's turn comes, I feel my anxiety rise again, and my heart pounds. She can't stand, so she sits up straight in a low beach chair on the grass. She is wearing a big white hat and white sunglasses that might have been appropriate for a sail around the Bahamas.

"Thanks for allowing me to speak of a special man who in my youth I adored, in my middle years respected, and in the last few years identified with," she reads from her pages.

Her voice is weak, and it's hard to hear as she reads. Birds in the branches and traffic on the distant parkway almost drown her out. I find myself wondering how many pages she has written, and pray it isn't many. Then I lower my head and listen to her remember my father.

"His sense of play was endless and magical and it dissolved all boredom and anxiety," she reads. "And he had a profound talent for relating to children."

As she laughs about feeding the ducks with him at Argyle Lake in Babylon and at his spectacular patience when he tried to teach her his beloved game of tennis, I find myself falling backward forty years, remembering holiday dinners and dressing her up in costumes to sing for our parents in living room shows. We were close, cousins who knew each other like siblings, and whose childhoods were full of birthday mischief, private games, and sleepovers. My father was part of it all, letting us dress him up and put him in our skits and movies.

"He embraced his inner child in so many healthy ways," Julie reads as the wind almost takes her pages. She grips them tighter. By now the crowd has stepped in closer to hear her. "And even when I no longer wanted to sing, and he didn't either, he'd get me to sing with him on the phone. He reminded me that there are many ways to sing and to do good in the world."

She is making the speech I wish I'd been able to make, the speech all of us wish we could make for people we love. What she's saying about our father is so potent and true that tears cover my face and my nose runs so much that I imagine my father rising up from his coffin to offer me a lint-covered tissue, or a spritz from his nose spray. How has my cousin Julie managed to capture him so well? How could I not have trusted her to carry the day for him and for all of us? I feel as sorry about my doubt as I feel proud of her. When she finishes, we remain silent for a long time. Nobody wants to go on. To go on means it's time to say the final good-bye. But we have to. We say our blessings and we shovel dirt on his grave in the Jewish tradition until he is covered. Julie's speech has given us the permission to leave him there beside my mother to rest in peace for their eternity.

Julie's own ending comes six months later, and it is a prolonged and terrible death. She wastes and weakens, but keeps her dignity and cheer to the end. Although she has read plenty about passing over to the next world, she has a hard time getting used to the idea of letting go of her life. "I thought I'd be prepared, but I'm not," she tells me one afternoon when I am visiting her on the couch in her living room, where she spends the last months under a cheery pink sequined cap to hide the pallor and baldness. She is alone that day. It almost seems that her family has been moving on without her, and that she knows it. But that's how families cope—with an unspoken letting go long before the actual death. It eases the pain of the final parting.

"This is the hardest thing I've ever done," she tells me.

When I think of Julie now, I hear her lilting high voice and remember the vulnerability in her large brown eyes as she sings, ripe with emotion. Then I remember my mother's face as well, and see her listening to Julie with pride as she leads the responsive singing at Sabbath services and family Seders. Around Father's Day each year, I take Julie's speech out and read it to myself. The typewritten pages are marked with her notes, indicating an unfinished process, a project not quite complete, ending with a last sentence that trails off without a period at the end, much the way her life ended too soon. Inevitably, images of my father fill my head, ending with a last one that is especially vivid. It's of him sitting up in his hospital bed, raising his hands to the ceiling and the heavens beyond.

"Wonderful!" he yells.

Acknowledgments

Thanks to Deb Futter at Twelve, who had faith in a tough subject; her savvy associate, Libby Burton; and inspired art director Catherine Casalino. Jay Mandel, Anna DeRoy, and Erin Conroy at William Morris Endeavor for taking the little piggy to market. Lou Ann Walker, Bob Reeves, and Susan Merrell at the *Southampton Review*, and Trip Gabriel and John Glassie at the *New York Times* for publishing early essays. Maira Kalman for egging me on. Suzanne Donaldson and Brittany Cutrone for the extra eyes. Mandy Morrison, Dan Shaw, and Barbara van Blarcum, my generous first responders. Amy Nederlander, Lucinda Rosenfeld, Liz Tuccillo, Jesse Oxfeld, Tracy Dockray Rudd, Susan Goldfarb, Dan Matthews, and Elisa Schappell for sharing stories. Janet Olshansky, my sister-in-law, who, like my brother and Aunt Bev, gracefully endures the privacy breaches. And to my husband, Ira Silverberg, who helps me find the emotion in every page and lets me imagine with something like humor, if not pleasure, the waning years ahead.

About the Author

Bob Morris is the author of *Crispin the Terrible* and *Assisted Loving*, which received honors from the American Library Association and Lambda Literary Awards, and was a *New York Times* editor's choice. A frequent contributor to the *Times*, he has also been a commentator for NPR's *All Things Considered* and has written for *The Southampton Review*, *Elle*, the *New Yorker*, *Town and Country*, and other publications. His comic plays have been produced off Broadway and he collaborated with actress Diahann Carroll on her award-winning memoir, *The Legs Are the Last to Go*. He is a graduate of Brown University and has a masters in creative writing from Stony Brook Southampton. He lives with his husband, Ira, and their dog, Zoloft, in Manhattan and Bellport, NY.

ABOUT TWELVE

TWELVE

TWELVE was established in August 2005 with the objective of publishing no more than twelve books each year. We strive to publish the singular book, by authors who have a unique perspective and compelling authority. Works that explain our culture; that illuminate, inspire, provoke, and entertain. We seek to establish communities of conversation surrounding our books. Talented authors deserve attention not only from publishers, but from readers as well. To sell the book is only the beginning of our mission. To build avid audiences of readers who are enriched by these works—that is our ultimate purpose.

For more information about forthcoming TWELVE books, please go to www.twelvebooks.com.